CASES IN CORRECTIONS

CASES IN CORRECTIONS

Michael Braswell
East Tennessee State University

Tyler Fletcher
University of Southern Mississippi

Goodyear Publishing Company, Inc., Santa Monica, California

Library of Congress Cataloging in Publication Data

BRASWELL, MICHAEL.
  Cases in corrections.

  Includes bibliographies.
    1. Corrections—United States—Case studies.
  2. Criminal justice, Administration of—United States—
  Case studies. I. Fletcher, Tyler, joint author.
  II. Title.
  HV9304.B72   364.6'0973   79-25043
  ISBN 0-8302-1310-4

Copyright © 1980 by Goodyear Publishing Company, Inc.
Santa Monica, California 90401

All rights reserved. No part of this book may be reproduced in any form or by any means without permission in writing from the publisher.

Current printing (last digit):

10 9 8 7 6 5 4 3 2 1

ISBN: 0-8302-1310-4
Y-1310-5

Printed in the United States of America

Designer: Linda M. Robertson

Production Editor: Nancy H. Carter

To Our Wives
SUSAN and SHIRLEY

Contents

SECTION **IV** **THE INMATE** **95**

READING
"Reality Therapy: Helping People Help Themselves" 177
RICHARD L. RACHIN

Case 1   **Anyone Want a Job?**   191
The State Board of Corrections is under pressure to hire
a qualified Corrections Commissioner, but politics
keep getting in the way.

Case 2   **Who's Running the Prison?**   195
When he was appointed as superintendent a year ago,
no one said anything about politics running the prison.
Yet the Superintendent is faced with constant political
interference in hiring practices and prison policy. What
does he do?

Case 3   **A Hostage Has Been Taken!**   199
The Superintendent is notified that some inmates have
taken an officer hostage, and have issued a list of
demands. What does he do?

Case 4   **Prison Sexuality**   201
A newly appointed prison Superintendent attempts to
deal effectively with an escalating number of sexual
assaults in his facility.

Case 5   **Managing a Women's Prison**   203
The new female Superintendent of the state women's
prison is confronted with the challenge of alleviating
substandard conditions. Since the women's prison
represents only ten percent of the state's inmate
population, the Commissioner is reluctant to help and
will have to be persuaded to provide the necessary
assistance.

Case 6   **Businessperson or Correctional**   205
         Administrator?
A halfway house Director is faced with financial and
other operational crises after a year of operation.

Preface

The intention of this book is to provide persons with the opportunity to identify with various roles involved in the correctional process. The roles of the inmate, correctional officer, law enforcement officer, prison administrator, and others comprise vital relationships that enhance or inhibit the correctional process. Understanding and gaining insight into these roles can help an individual to more effectively relate to the offender and to professional peers. It is the authors' contention that effective relationships are the major contributors to correctional successes. Such relationships can create an effective system, and not vice versa.

Michael Braswell
Tyler Fletcher

Acknowledgement

Many students and professional colleagues in academic and agency settings provided valuable input regarding the development of this book. Of special mention are H. T. Cox, Don Cabana, and Ron Jones.

We are especially indebted to Jack Pritchard of Goodyear Publishing Company for giving us the opportunity to go forward with our idea, and to Tom Phelps of California State University at Sacramento for providing us with meaningful suggestions for improving the final project.

Finally, we wish to thank Vickie Beam, Carol Barger, and William Workman for their typing and editorial assistance.

M.B.
T.F.

LAW ENFORCEMENT AND CORRECTIONS

The following five cases and reading are designed to enable you to better understand the correctional impact of the law enforcement officer, particularly in the area of "preventive" corrections. The deterrent potential of the police officer's discretionary arrest powers, the educational and preventive possibilities in speaking to elementary school children, and the need for interpersonal effectiveness in dealing with community squabbles suggest that law enforcement professionals have implicit secondary correctional responsibilities in conjunction with their traditional enforcement duties. Although community relations programs can contribute to preventive corrections, jail programs have a more direct correctional impact.

As you react to the next five cases and try to develop solutions to the problems presented, you should make an effort to view each case from the perspective of a law enforcement officer so that you can better understand their relationship to the correctional process.

A reading on how police officers handle disputes and conflicts in the community is included at the end of this section.

Discretionary Arrest

You have been out of the police academy for about a year and have been assigned to a mobile unit patrolling the outskirts of the city. You are working the graveyard shift and have found it to be inconsistent, either very busy or very quiet, no in between.

Your area consists principally of all-night cafes, truck stops, a bowling alley with a very active lounge, several second class motels, and a few bars that cater to transients. The road net is excellent, and because there are a great many speed violations, any accidents which occur are usually serious. Otherwise the highways and roads into the city are pretty quiet, and a good place for a new police officer's first solo assignment.

One night about 3:30, you are making your regular rounds which include checking the bowling alley. The alley and the lounge have been closed since 1:00 A.M., but you notice two cars parked in the rear of the bowling alley parking lot. Upon closer inspection you see that one automobile has two occupants and the second car appears to be empty. You drive alongside the occupied vehicle, and without getting out of your patrol car you question the two occupants, a male and a female, both middle aged. From the looks of things, you conclude that you have interrupted a romantic rendezvous instead of a potential burglary; both are busily adjusting their clothing and the smell of alcohol is quite noticeable. You decide not to check the vehicle but tell the occupants that they are on private property without the owner's permission and advise them to "finish their conversation and go home." You note the license plate numbers and continue your rounds.

About 4:30 A.M., you decide to return to the bowling alley parking lot to see if the two lovers have departed or if you had made a mistake and the bowling alley has been burglarized. As you expected, the two lovers have departed and the bowling alley seems secure.

A short distance from the bowling alley you receive a CB call about a traffic problem. Upon arrival at the scene you observe that a vehicle has run off the embankment of the highway, still has its lights on, and a second vehicle has also pulled off on the shoulder of the road. Traffic has slowed because of drivers looking at the accident. You recognize the vehicles as the same two that were at the bowling alley earlier. The two subjects now appear quite unsteady on their feet, and their speech is slurred when they answer your questions. In short, your two lovers sat in the car and got drunk instead of going home as you instructed. You feel some guilt that you did not remain on the scene at the initial contact to see that your advice was followed. Now you have no choice but to investigate the accident and take the subjects into custody.

You pick up the subjects' driver's licenses, check the license plates with the National Crime Information Center, and advise the radio operator of your action. Both violators apologize for not following your earlier advice, and show no undue reaction when you ask them to lock up their cars and accompany you in your patrol car to the police station. You confiscate their vehicle keys and decide not to frisk them. You advise the dispatcher and proceed directly to the station with your two offenders.

At the station the Breathalyzer test confirms your suspicions and each subject is charged with drunk driving and booked for the remainder of the night in jail.

At this time, the male subject approaches you and asks you to reconsider the charges. He states that you will find out he has a criminal record, is on parole, and is certain to be given a revocation hearing and returned to the penitentiary. In addition, the woman he is with is his boss's wife and if the boss finds out, he will lose his job the next day. She was supposedly spending the night with her sister.

You feel sympathetic. The subject is not belligerent, seems sincere, and you can truthfully say he was much easier to handle than any other drunk you have dealt with since you have been on the force. Furthermore, there is no reported damage to anyone's property, and the wrecker will probably be able to extricate the subject's vehicle easily the next day. You also feel a little guilty that if you had followed through earlier and gotten them on the road, the incident might not have occurred. You talk to the desk sergeant and he tells you, "It's your decision."

INSTRUCTIONS:

Decide on a course of action.

A. Carefully define the problem.
B. List all the options or choices you can think of.
C. Rank these options in order of priority.
D. Select the option that you think is the best and briefly discuss the probable consequences.

Law Enforcement and Elementary School

You remember vividly how you felt as a child when you saw a police officer. Even though you were usually well behaved, you felt a sense of awe and fear in the presence of a uniformed officer. As you grew up, a police officer continued to command your respect for the law out of simple fear. When an officer came to school to talk with your class, everyone sat up straight in their chairs and no one made any noise. Your behavior was much better than for your teacher, who was the real authority figure at the school.

When the officer spoke, he seemed nice enough, but you always thought there was something that made him different from other men such as your dad. Whatever the reason, you know that you always trembled slightly at the sight of a police officer.

Now it is twenty years later. You made it through school and young adulthood without any major problems. You married your college sweetheart and have a nine-year-old son. Your life is stable and you have settled on a career. You are a police officer in your home town. You have just begun your eighth year on the force and you are about to begin a new assignment—community relations. To enhance the community relations program, your police chief has revived the practice of visiting the schools and talking with the kids. On the way to your first speaking engagement, you remember how proud the officer looked when he spoke to you as a kid. He commanded respect and attention . . . and fear.

You have made sure that your uniform and patrol car look sharp in order to present a good appearance. When you walk into the classroom, you receive an unpleasant surprise. Instead of sitting up straight and taking notice of you, the class seems disinterested; some students are talking and others are looking out the window. You begin to wonder what is going to happen. You had expected to be an instant success! Your introduction to the class brings no change. You begin to talk, but the class is not responding. You have invited the class to ask questions at any time. One eight-year-old who has been talking to another student raises his hand and asks, "Why do you want to be a pig?" You might have expected this out of a seventeen-year-old who has had a conflict with the police, but not out of an eight-year old boy.

You are really shaken by the eight-year-old's description of the police and the general attitude of the class. You pull yourself together enough to mumble some answer about pride in your job and serving people. You are at a loss for words; you were not expecting this kind of reaction.

You want to find some way to interest, motivate, and communicate with the class. You do not want to leave with negative feelings between you and the kids. You want children to understand that police officers are friends and not "pigs." How do you do it?

INSTRUCTIONS:

Decide on a course of action.

A. Carefully define the problem.
B. List all the options or choices you can think of.
C. Rank these options in order of priority.
D. Select the option that you think is the best and briefly discuss the probable consequences.

Family Crisis Intervention

You are a twenty-two-year-old patrolwoman. You enjoy your job because it has both variety and excitement. You are completing your first year of work which comprises a probationary period with the police department in which you are employed. You graduated high in your academy class and are learning from experience quickly. Your supervising partner is a seventeen-year veteran who is highly respected and looks forward to retirement in three years. During your short tour of duty, you have noticed the extreme cautiousness of your partner. You believe in being as safe as possible, but you are beginning to feel that your partner's caution has interfered with doing a complete job in some instances.

During one particular night shift, your unit received a family disturbance call from a poorer section of the city. Being a graduate of a modern police school, you knew the inherent danger of these types of calls and the need to resolve the problem the first time you go to the residence. Each time you return to a family disturbance, the danger increases. The section of town involved in this call had a reputation for violence. When you arrived at the location, you were eager to reach the scene, which was a third floor apartment. You arrived at the apartment before your partner; this was a mistake, but you felt your partner did not respond as quickly as the situation warranted. When you entered the residence, a verbal confrontation between a middle-aged couple was taking place. Observing the female, you saw that she had been severely beaten. Concerned for her safety, you felt that she should sign a complaint authorizing you to arrest the male. As you attempted to convince the woman to sign the complaint, the man repeatedly tried to override your message. Nevertheless, you were able to maintain control of the situation. Just as the woman was about to sign the complaint, your partner arrived. "What's going on?" he asked. The woman explained that she was about to sign a complaint. Your partner interrupted her, saying, "Lady, you don't want your husband to go to jail, do you?" She began crying and subsequently decided not to sign the complaint. Even though you felt her personal safety was threatened, there was little you could do because the assault was not committed in your presence. You remained quiet even though you were steaming inside. As you prepared to leave your partner gave the couple the typical warning about quieting down because of neighbors.

You are not especially upset at the final results of the call, because most of the time a warning is all that can be given in a situation like the one you and your partner had just experienced. However, you are upset with your partner for not backing you up in your chosen course of action. As you see it, you have two choices: one is to talk with your partner and try to persuade him to become more assertive when dealing with family disturbances; the other is to ask to be assigned to a new partner. Neither choice seems to have much promise. You have tried to talk with your partner before and you feel that he will never change; all he seems to want is to retire without any trouble. If you request a new partner, he could be even worse. At the very least, you would be putting down a well-respected veteran police officer. In your short time on the force, you have seen several young officers get into trouble with the department for trying to knock an older cop. Even though you feel you have a legitimate complaint, your age and experience will probably work against you, while your partner is referred to as "one of the best in the business." Something has to be done to create better cooperation between you and your partner. The problem is how to do it without making too many waves.

INSTRUCTIONS:

Decide on a course of action.

- A. Carefully define the problem.
- B. List all the options or choices you can think of.
- C. Rank these options in order of priority.
- D. Select the option that you think is the best and briefly discuss the probable consequences.

Crime Prevention and the Community

A church related citizens' group has approached the police chief about the problem of repeat offenders and has proposed a church sponsored group home for offenders who are to be released on parole and need a place of residence.

You are a newly assigned member of the police crime prevention unit. Since your sergeant is on summer vacation, the chief calls you in for a conference. He wants to talk over with you the idea of the group home before he makes a commitment to the citizens' group.

You feel flattered that the chief would ask your advice on such an issue. The whole proposition that concerned citizens would approach the department with a scheme to reduce crime sounds like a first class community relations project. Citizen involvement, no monetary costs to the department, the possibility of reduction of recidivism with consequent reduction of crime—the situation sounds too good to be true.

As the chief describes the proposed project to you, you can hardly hide your enthusiasm until the chief comes to the bottom line. "I'm against it. There are enough criminals in this community without inviting a group of proven undesirables into town to make matters worse." The chief cites the well-known statistic about criminal acts and the repeater, and concludes the conversation by telling you to think it over and let him know your feelings on the subject the next day. "After all," the chief says, "it is going to be your job to deal with those people one way or another."

You agree with the chief and return to your office to ponder the situation. Crime prevention is built through better police-community relations, but how do you foster community support to prevent crimes, keep the chief happy, and yet turn down a program sponsored by the community that may be the key to community relations success?

You decide to seek the advice of your old patrol sergeant, Joe Green, to learn how the operating line officer would react to the proposal. Joe has a real "feel" for what is going on in the community and ought to be able to help you formulate a position on the matter.

After thirteen years in the patrol division, Joe Green has developed a feeling for people's attitudes that is close to ESP. He can sense change and seems to perceive danger before it ever surfaces. He is seldom mistaken when it comes to predicting how people will react to a given situation, and he is widely respected for his perceptive ability.

Sergeant Green was characteristically thoughtful about the project, "You don't get that kind of citizens' involvement very often," he said. "It shows they really want to do something. But I'll be damned if I would want to encourage criminals to come into the community for any reason, even if it is to live in a monastery. You know how these guys on parole are; they all have their fingers in some type of criminal activity, or else they are on welfare. And the parole officers, that's a laugh. Those jokers are responsible for so many parolees that all they do is fill out papers. I'll bet you the parole officer can't even tell you where half his cases are, except by reading the reports the parolees drop by his office once a month." Sergeant Green was right on that point. The only time the parolee actually came face to face with his parole officer was upon release or on a pick up for a violation. Sergeant Green continued thoughtfully, "This community relations stuff is all right, but I would rather see all those 'do gooders' rechannel their efforts and keep their kids off the street at night or improve the job possibilities for the kids that have nothing to do, instead of fooling around with a bunch of hoods who are probably going to turn around and commit the same criminal act again." Green was quiet, but firm; "I agree with the chief," he concluded.

You are almost convinced, but to complete the matter you decide to talk to Rev. Millhouse, pastor of the church whose congregation made the proposal.

Rev. Millhouse is right to the point. He heard your supervisor speak at the Lions Club luncheon last month and call for citizen support; he considers the group home an appropriate response. If his congregation will support the project, give some ex-felons a break by providing a decent place to live and some help with a job, Rev. Millhouse thinks there will be a good chance to reduce the crime rate. Even if the reduction is slight, he is convinced the project will be worthwhile. "You see," says Rev. Millhouse, "it is really your idea we are following."

You return to your office to review the situation. You have a couple of hours before your late afternoon appointment with the chief. You think you know what you are going to say.

INSTRUCTIONS:

Decide on a course of action.

A. Carefully define the problem.
B. List all the options or choices you can think of.
C. Rank these options in order of priority.
D. Select the option that you think is the best and briefly discuss the probable consequences.

Corrections in Jail

You have just received your Bachelor of Science degree in Law Enforcement. The curriculum included some courses in corrections as well as the law enforcement core, so your first job in the jail section of the sheriff's office is not completely alien to you. You feel you have enough basic knowledge to get by, and you are looking forward to the assignment.

The sheriff has three chief deputies: one for criminal activity, one for civil process, and one for the jail. The sheriff requires all new deputies to start in the jail section and work their way into the criminal division where the action is. The jail division has a number of ''old-timers''—men who want those ''eight to five'' duty hours and who are, perhaps, a little too old for the street. But the jailers wear uniforms just like the other deputies, and there is no way to tell the difference when you walk out of the jail section and onto the street. The division also has a retired female licensed practical nurse. All things considered, the day shift in the jail is pretty routine although there is usually some some excitement on weekends.

The jail itself is almost new, having been financed for the most part by Law Enforcement Assistance Administration funds. However, it has no recreational facility or any significant community oriented programs. Therefore a stay in jail is a stay in custody with very little physical or mental activity. The chief deputy for the jail has initiated his own trustee system in which certain adult prisoners are released to work during the day with little or no supervision. They usually clean up the offices in the jail and the court house and wash county cars. Most of the female prisoners work in the kitchen. Those who are new and are not known to the jailers are not released except to walk around the exercise area twice a day.

Your first few weeks pass rapidly and you begin to settle into the routine. However, you are concerned about the waste of manpower caused by not letting more of the prisoners out to work. As you see it, few are dangerous or likely to escape; few are misdemeanants, and many of the offenders are not convicted, but simply awaiting trial because they could not make bail. There are a few who are awaiting grand jury action and could be classified as "pretty tough customers." There are also a few local inmates who are serving out their sentences in the jail.

You decide to approach the chief deputy to see if some sort of voluntary work release program could be devised to get some of the prisoners out in the day and have them return at night. You reason that it would save the county money on meals and give the prisoners some sense of self-worth and accomplishment. A prisoner might even be able to make enough to cover the 10 percent required by the bail bondsman.

The chief deputy for corrections had two pieces of advice when you brought up the subject to him. "Wait till you've been here longer before you bring up ideas like that. And if you don't like it here, go see the sheriff." He was sincere about what he said, too. He had been with the sheriff for seven years, ever since his retirement from the military service. He had carefully formulated his jail regulations to require ease of supervision, the least probability of escape, and the fewest entanglements with lawyers, citizen groups, and the grand jury. Since ease of supervision required restricted movement, the chief deputy's policy was to keep the prisoners in their cells as much as possible and call it "tight security." The other quality his reputation rested on was cleanliness. The jail was spotless and any visitors, including the grand jury, usually commented favorably on its condition and appearance. In fact, most visitors deduced that if the jail was clean, it was well managed; and for the record, one escape in the last two years spoke for itself. The chief deputy was pretty smart all right.

You considered his advice. If the sheriff thinks the idea is good, the chief deputy will undoubtedly accept it. But if it involves a greater risk of having a prisoner walk off, if it involves some degree of community acceptance, and if it involves some planning and legwork with prospective employers, the chief deputy will never really accept it.

You must decide whether or not to draw up a plan and present it to the sheriff, recognizing that his decision would concern more than just the proposal you would be submitting.

INSTRUCTIONS:

Decide on a course of action.

A. Carefully define the problem.
B. List all the options or choices you can think of.
C. Rank these options in order of priority.
D. Select the option that you think is the best and briefly discuss the probable consequences.

How Police Handle Explosive Squabbles New Techniques Let Police Settle Arguments Without Force

Morton Bard and

Joseph Zacker

Police officers have to deal with disputes and arguments every day of the year. Thus the world of the police is an excellent laboratory in which to study the origins and dynamics of human conflict. What psychologists know about such conflict comes mostly from lab experiments and game theory, and among the few places where they have studied passionate disputes have been the courtroom and the labor-management negotiating table. But close at hand, in every community, an opportunity exists for behavioral scientists to observe human beings in conflict situations.

Disputes are among the most dangerous assignments for police officers. A family squabble can turn into a three-party nightmare of violence and irrationality. An argument in a bar between friends, or on a stairwell between a landlord and tenant, can become a shootout. About 25 percent of all police officers killed in the line of duty are intervening in a dispute. It is estimated that about 40 percent of police injuries result from the same thankless task.

Despite the public's growing awareness of how much time police devote to disputes—and despite a good deal of professional interest in training officers to handle them more effectively—most people still accept as facts what are really only myths about small-scale conflicts. Two of these supposed facts are that most disputes are actually drunken brawls, and that there is a direct relationship between alcohol and assaultiveness. These assumptions are deeply ingrained in the minds of police officers. They are also widely accepted by most behavioral scientists and sound equally plausible to the layman as well.

But they may not be true, and the way we discovered the facts of the matter was by working with groups of policemen in New York City and Norwalk, Connecticut, who systematically recorded thousands of interventions into all kinds of arguments. The common view that alcohol and assaultiveness are causally linked is only

Reprinted from Psychology Today Magazine, Copyright © 1976 Ziff-Davis Publishing Company, November, 1976.

one of several preconceptions we have examined during nine years of naturalistic research into police-managed interpersonal conflicts.

People call the police for help in an incredible variety of conflicts, but particularly in family disturbances. As Tolstoy said in *Anna Karenina:* "Happy families are all alike, each unhappy family is unhappy in its own way." Men fight with women and parents fight with their children, and some of these fights end in death. In New York City, for example, during 1974, 54 husbands killed their wives, 42 wives killed their husbands, and at least 77 other people killed their parents, children, brothers or sisters. Similar killings occur elsewhere in the nation, in rural areas as well as in urban settings.

It is true, as reported recently in the press, that the proportion of people who are killed by total strangers has been increasing lately. But an American is still more likely to be a homicide victim of a relative or friend than of a stranger. The scenes of most murders are kitchens and bedrooms, parties and parking lots.

NO LOVE WITHOUT AGGRESSION

Significantly, some of the key theorists in the social and behavioral sciences, who often hold differing opinions, agree that personal closeness leads to intense antagonism and sometimes to violence. The turn-of-the-century social theorist George Simmel, for instance, emphasized that intimate social relations were unavoidably aggressive. Sigmund Freud, during his earlier theorizing, contended that aggression was more socially reactive than biologically instinctive. Anthropologist Bronislaw Malinowski charted a similar channel between close social contact and aggression; and most recently, several prominent ethologists have discovered the same tendency among nonhuman animals. As Konrad Lorenz puts it: "intraspecific aggression can certainly exist without its counterpart, love, but conversely there is no love without aggression." In short, the theorists agree with the statistics that conflicts between individuals—the flesh-and-blood arguments that often involve the police—spring up typically among friends, acquaintances, and relatives rather than among strangers.

This general rule may help explain one of the most interesting recent findings of our own research into disputes: white people generally fight with whites, and blacks tend to fight with other blacks. More curious than that, however, is that an interracial dispute managed by the police is less likely to result in assaultiveness than a dispute between members of the same race. We found this to be so from an analysis of dozens of interracial arguments, all of which resulted in a call to the police but relatively few of which resulted in an actual assault.

Among other interesting facts about disputes which have evolved from our studies are the following:

1. Disputes are not as assaultive as most people, including the police, tend to assume. One might think that any family argument serious enough to require the cops would necessarily be violent. But it's not true. Out of 1,388 family disturbance calls answered by policemen participating in our West Harlem study, only 36 percent of the complainants reported an actual assault, and the officers on duty felt that some of those complaints were false. Physical violence is the exception rather than

the rule, even in those family arguments that wind up with an officer at the door.

These findings with the New York City Police Department were supported by similar studies with the New York City Housing Authority police and with the Norwalk police. Many of the disputes in the Norwalk study did not involve families and yet yielded similar findings.

2. As we mentioned earlier, disputes are caused by all sorts of problems. The same applies to family disputes that involve assault. As one might expect, suspicion or conviction of a spouse's infidelity is one of the most common reasons for an assaultive family argument; yet even this reason accounts for only one in six cases of assault in our studies.

3. History is the best predictor of what's to come; assaults are most common in families that have engaged in assaultive behavior in the past.

4. The police rarely resort to physical force in dealing with family disputes.

In principle, any number of people might intervene in a dispute and try to separate and/or pacify the disputants. (There must be thousands of cases each day in this country in which friends, neighbors, and even total strangers handle conflicts between people.) But it would be naive to think we can depend on those solutions alone. The police are used when an authority is required who is legally empowered to do *something* "here and now"—that is, to prevent destructive escalation or to restore social order.

NATIVE INSIGHTS

A father may call the police because his roving son won't listen to him. Two neighbors may engage in a dispute over their property line. A landlord and tenant may dispute over nonpayment of rent. A storekeeper may argue with a customer over the exchange of merchandise. Two motorists may get into an altercation over a minor traffic accident. In every case, the officers who arrive are expected to manage the problem.

Traditionally, the police have been seen as trying to take charge by using force. In any event, that's the stereotype of police behavior and there may even be some truth in it. Our data from the Norwalk study, however, suggest that most police officers spontaneously develop and use subtle intervention tactics despite their lack of formal training. They have relied on their experiences both in uniform and out, and on their native insights into human problems.

But the police can also play it strictly by the book, and in the past many officers have assumed that professional behavior should be that of the professional soldier—one who takes orders from above and gives orders to those below. However, such attitudes cannot be relied on exclusively. There is a need for flexibility and choice in selecting an approach to a problem that is appropriate to the circumstances.

During the last ten years, various new techniques of interpersonal conflict management have worked their way into police departments across the country. To a great extent they reflect changes in American attitudes generally, or a shift away from authoritarian approaches toward those of mediation, arbitration, and other means of conflict management.

This may strike some obsevers as wishy-washy and "liberal," or, alternatively, as manipulative and "totalitarian," but conflict-management techniques are inherently neither. We have found that they have been measurably effective in reducing some forms of crime, in helping people who would have no other resources, and in reducing police injuries and deaths.

In one program after another, officers have been trained in basic psychology and sociology, in the nature of aggression, in social relations, and in methods of keeping people calm. They have also learned that other systems can often serve the needs of people in conflict in more constructive ways than can the criminal justice system. Other systems that are often more relevant are mental health and social services.

We have participated in programs involving officers in two New York City police departments (the New York Police Department and the Housing Authority Police Department) as well as in the Norwalk, Connecticut, Department of Police Services. Two of these projects emphasized interpersonal effectiveness in dealing with disputes; the third emphasized participatory data gathering and analysis in dealing with police-managed interpersonal disputes. All three projects involved psychologists and officers working together as equals. Much, in fact, of what we have been able to say about interpersonal conflict could not have been learned without the committed participation of the officers who took part in these programs. We contributed our knowledge in psychology while they contributed their knowledge in law enforcement.

1,388 DISTURBANCES

Our first effort was in West Harlem, where eighteen police officers participated in a demonstration project to determine the possibility of improving the police management of family disputes. There were lectures, workshops, and a series of real-life simulations in which the officers could practice various kinds of professional interventions. We were trying to discover the kinds of attitudes and issues that are inimical to successful interventions. Following this preliminary phase, the Family Crisis Unit went into the street, where it functioned in general police work—except that the unit was assigned all family disputes in the precinct. The officers both used their evolving skills and systematically recorded everything that happened.

The demonstration period of twenty-two months yielded promising results. The eighteen officers processed 1,388 disturbances involving 962 families, and there was no known homicide in any of those families during the entire period. Nor were any officers injured, despite a statistical probability that they should have been. Arrests for assault went down in the precinct, and confidence in the police apparently went up. The officers performed their specialized role extremely well, but most important, there appeared to be a spillover in the performance of *all* their police duties. This was confirmed in the Housing Authority study, where we found that the general level of performance of Housing Authority officers who had been trained in conflict management was significantly superior to that of other officers in two control groups.

In 1973, we conducted a related study in Norwalk, Connecticut, where we expanded our view of interpersonal conflict to include arguments among acquaintances and strangers as well as among relatives. In Norwalk we were dealing with a much more middle-class community than we had in black, working-class West Harlem; the average family income was more than $12,000, and only 12 percent of the residents were nonwhite. Yet another twist was that in Norwalk, the officers developed a basis for a training program by systematically recording their own, spontaneously developed, ways of managing conflicts. A panel of five officers and four psychologists organized and studied the results.

What the Norwalk officers gained from this experience was more than a group of techniques for handling conflicts, although they certainly learned some of those as they evaluated their own behavior. They also gained a more objective and systematic body of knowledge of what conflicts are all about and how policemen handle them.

The officers found that they used a greater variety of approaches than they had believed. They also discovered that some of the approaches were used because they were more appropriate in certain situations. For example, mediation is a technique that officers use many times and in many subtle ways. Sometimes they separate the disputants and conduct a kind of shuttle diplomacy from room to room. In other cases they try to articulate the point of view of an inarticulate disputant, or lay down rules for discussion and then act as a referee.

Other broad types of intervention that the Norwalk police were already using were the authoritative approach and the counseling approach. An officer relying on his authority as an agent of the law might threaten arrest or simply order people to comply. These approaches do have their usefulness, particularly when disputants are enraged, intoxicated, or otherwise disordered. Counseling, on the other hand, may work best when the disputants are fairly calm and lucid, or when there is clearly some underlying problem that the officer is able to identify and explain.

CONTRADICTING OLD CLICHÉS

One of the officers had trouble accepting some of the study's findings even though he had participated in the data collection and analysis. He was unable to relinquish his own bias even in the face of facts that he had helped discover. For example: two-thirds of the 344 disputes managed in Norwalk, according to the panel's analysis of the officers' reports, involved *no* drinking by either party. This is an important finding, since we had always assumed (as do most officers) that alcohol is a crucial factor in conflicts among people. Further, there was no relationship between the use of alcohol and assaultiveness. This finding contradicts the long-standing assumptions of both police officers and social scientists. We are now reasonably convinced of its accuracy, having reached the same finding in our Harlem studies.

We also learned that assaultiveness in these disputes was related to a person's social and economic class but not to his or her race. Blacks, in other words, are no more or less apt to assault an antagonist than are whites. But the poorer a disputant is, the more likely he or she is to become assaultive. According to the reports of Norwalk's officer-researchers, less than 30 percent of the cases in which the disputants were middle class or wealthy ended in an assault, whereas there were assaults in 44 percent of the conflicts in which the disputants were poor.

This finding won't surprise those who have suspected all along that there is something about poverty that leads to personal aggression. But it may surprise those who believe that certain ethnic traditions are prone to violence.

The naturalistic studies we have talked about here are hardly as rigorous as laboratory experiments, yet they have obvious advantages. For one thing, they have produced a good deal of information about interpersonal conflicts, and that information is valuable in itself. Some of it, in fact, strongly contradicts the findings of laboratory experiments—such as those with rats that show a direct relationship between alcohol and aggression. Assaultiveness and drinking aren't nearly so closely related in the world, apparently.

More important, though, these studies focus on urgent public problems. The police have to deal with the kinds of fights we've been talking about every day and night of the year, and they are some of the most potentially dangerous and unpredictable events in a police officer's life. What we've tried to do by collaborating with police officers in "action research" is to make those scenes less dangerous, more predictable, and less damaging to the antagonists involved.

These same studies, meanwhile, offer psychologists an opportunity to add to our knowledge of human behavior by refining methods for research where the action is. In addition, they demonstrate how psychology can participate in solving real problems—in the present case, through a method of preventive mental health and crime prevention.

NOTES

For more information, read:

1. Bard, Morton. "The Naturalistic Study of Conflict and Violence." Paper presented at symposium, American Association for the Advancement of Science, Boston, Mass., Feb. 24, 1976.
2. Bard, Morton and Joseph Zacker. "The Police and Interpersonal Conflict: Third-Party Intervention Approaches," Police Foundation, 1909 K St. N.W., Washington, D.C. 20006, Sept. 1976.
3. Sullivan, Ronald. "Violence, Like Charity, Begins at Home," in New York Times Magazine. Nov. 24, 1968.
4. Zacker, Joseph and Morton Bard. "Effects of Conflict Management Training on Police Performance" in Journal of Applied Psychology, 1973, Vol. 58, No. 2, pp. 202-208.
5. Zacker, Joseph and Morton Bard. "Further Findings on Assaultiveness and Alcohol Use in Interpersonal Disputes" in American Journal of Community Psychology, in press.

Selected Bibliography

BARD, MORTON. *The Function of the Police in Crisis Intervention and Conflict management*. U.S. Government Printing Office, U.S. Department of Justice, 1975.

BARD, MORTON. *Training Police As Specialists in Family Crisis Intervention*. U.S. Government Printing Office, U.S. Department of Justice, May, 1970.

BRESLIN, WARREN J. "Police Intervention in Domestic Confrontations." *Journal of Police Science and Administration*, 6(3):293–302, 1978.

COFFEY, ALLEN; ELDEFONSO, EDWARD; and HARTINGER, WALTER. *Human Relations: Law Enforcement in a Changing Community*. Englewood Cliffs, New Jersey: Prentice Hall, 1971.

COHN, ALVIN W., and VIANO, EMILIO C. *Police Community Relations: Images, Roles, Realities*. Philadelphia: J.B. Lippincott Co., 1976.

ELDEFONSO, EDWARD. *Law Enforcement and the Youthful Offender*. 2d ed., New York: John Wiley and Sons, 1973.

GOLDSTEIN, ARNOLD P.; MONTI, PHILIP J.; SARDINO, THOMAS J.; and GREEN, DONALD J. *Police Crisis Intervention*. Kalamazoo, Michigan: Behaviordelia, 1977.

LEWIS, RODNEY. "Toward an Understanding of Police Anomie." *Journal of Police Science and Administration*, 1(1973):484–490.

LOFTUS, ELIZABETH F.; ALTMAN, DIANE; and GEBALLE, ROBERT. "Effects of Questioning Upon a Witness' Later Recollections." *Journal of Police Science and Administration*, 3(1975):162–165.

KERBER. W; ANDES, STEVEN: and MITTLER, MICHELE B. "Citizen Attitudes Regarding the Competence of Female Police Officers." *Journal of Police Science and Administration*, 5(1977):337–347.

KENNEDY, DANIEL B. *The Dysfunctional Alliance*. Cincinnati: Anderson Publishing Co., 1977.

KLEIN, MALCOLM W.; ROSENSWEIG, SUSAN LABIN; and BATES, RONALD. "The Ambiguous Juvenile Arrest." *Criminology,* 13(1975):78–89.

MANNING, PETER K., and VAN MAANEN, JOHN (eds.), *Policing: A View From The Street.* Santa Monica, Calif.: Goodyear Publishing Co., 1978.

MUNRO, JIM L. *Administrative Behavior and Police Organization.* Cincinnati: W. H. Anderson Co., 1974.

PALMER, JOHN W. "Pre-Arrest Diversion: Victim Confrontation." *Federal Probation,* 38 (1974):12–18.

PRIMEAU, CAROL C. "An Examination of the Conception of the Police Officer Held by Several Social Groups." *Journal of Police Science and Administration,* 3(1975):189–96.

RATHBONE, DAVID L. "The Police As A Social Servant." *Journal of Humanics,* 4(1977):78–82.

RUSSELL, HAROLD E. and BEIGEL, ALLAN. *Understanding Human Behavior For Effective Police Work.* New York: Bosich Books, Inc., 1976.

RUSINKO, WILLIAM T.; JOHNSON, KNOWLTON W.; HORNING, CARLTON A. "The Importance of Police Contact in the Formulation of Youth's Attitudes Toward Police." *Journal of Criminal Justice,* 6(Spring, 1978): 53–69.

SCHAEFER, ROGER. "Law Enforcer, Peace Keeper, Servicer: Role Alternative for Policemen." *Journal of Police Science and Administration,* 6(1978):324–335.

SKOLNICK, JEROME H. *Justice Without Trial: Law Enforcement in Democratic Society,* 2d ed., New York: John Wiley and Sons, 1975.

SUNDEEN, RICHARD A. "Police Professionalization and Community Attachments and Diversions of Juveniles." *Criminology,* 11(February, 1974):570–580.

TENZEL, JAMES H.; STORMS, LOWELL; and SWEETWOOD, HARVEY. "Symbols and Behavior: An Experiment in Altering the Police Role." *Journal of Police Science and Administration,* 4(1976):21–27.

THE COURT
AND CORRECTIONS

The courts have a greater impact on corrections than perhaps any other component of the criminal justice system. Whether dealing with the civil rights of prison inmates or abused children, courts represent whatever parity that is to be found in our system of justice. In the next five cases and reading you will deal with problems from the viewpoint of court professionals. As a family court judge you will have to use your judicial discretion concerning a child abuse case. Other cases require deciding the appropriate purpose and limits of a presentence investigation and determining the consequences for a repeat juvenile offender.

Two readings on standardization of presentence reports are included at the end of the section.

Presentence Investigation: A Fair Shake?

The case was a shocking revelation in the community when the arrest was made by the State Bureau of Criminal Investigation. The sheriff had not even been aware that an investigation was under way, much less that such a prominent citizen as Johnny James was involved.

As you followed the trial, it became apparent that you would be given the presentence investigation. The outcome of the trial never seemed to be in doubt. Public indignation that a former state's attorney should be involved in receiving stolen property and disposing of it in conspiracy with a convicted felon was high. The stolen items, worth tens of thousands of dollars each, included heavy equipment stolen from construction sites which had been stashed out on the attorney's ranch and ultimately disposed of through a third party. It was a lucrative racket and probably would have gone undetected had not one of the buyers offered to sell a bulldozer back to the same contractor from whom it was stolen. The bulldozer was quickly identified by the rightful owner by an unusual mechanical modification that had been made before the equipment was stolen from a roadside work site. The resultant investigation revealed altered serial numbers and criminal intent.

You know that the presentence investigation is going to be tough. You will find those who are going to soften their criticism because of current associations with Johnny James, and those who want to "hang" him because they believe a public official, even an ex-public official, ought to set a moral example in the community and certainly not be a common "fence" for stolen goods.

The investigation progressed quickly and Johnny James was out on bail. James had been a fine high school athlete, and president of his class, and had attended the best law school in the state. He soon established himself as a smart lawyer and an ambitious and successful businessperson. Fifteen years later, he owned a controlling interest in a farm implement company, a thriving automobile business, and an interest in a large motel. He was considered a friend of law enforcement, hosting a large annual party for area law officers. He was also a model member of the community in most respects, with strong church affiliations and membership in several respected and prestigious civic organizations. His wife headed a local hospital volunteer effort and there was no indication of any rift within the family. Aside from strong contrasting opinions of local citizens, there was no indication of danger to the community if this particular offender continued to reside there.

However, one matter bothers you about this investigation. Why should this "big time" lawyer who has been involved in the theft of thousands of dollars worth of private property be out on bail, possibly never to serve a day of "hard time," while a more ordinary thief would no doubt receive a more traditional sentence in the state penitentiary? You feel that crime is crime, whether white collar or not.

You wonder if you should look deeper into Johnny James's background for indications of a pattern that might predict continued criminal behavior. Perhaps his campaign contributions and his political connections should also be investigated. You know for a fact his motel is frequented by out-of-town "hookers" who are never arrested. This kind of information could influence the judge and might even result in a prison sentence.

INSTRUCTIONS:

Decide on a course of action.

A. Carefully define the problem.
B. List all the options or choices you can think of.
C. Rank these options in order of priority.
D. Select the option that you think is the best and briefly discuss the probable consequences.

Diversion or Sentencing?

As a female correctional officer in charge of the women's section of the jail, you have seen the regular Saturday night customers arrive in a steady stream since about 10:00 P.M. You are surprised when the police book two attractive females in their early twenties who are apparently not the run-of-the-mill Saturday night drunks. You soon learn that they are students at the local college. One is charged with driving while intoxicated and the other with public drunkenness. Both are indignant, but you can see that they are probably legally drunk. Neither has the money or local connections to make bail. They are assigned to your section to await appearance before a magistrate on Monday.

From the charges, you gather that the two young women were in an automobile registered to the out-of-state parents of one of the girls. While they were sitting in the car in the parking lot of the "Emergency Room," a local bar and college hangout, the women made certain derogatory remarks to officers Tragden and Owens, who were making one of their frequent checks. The officers inspected the vehicle and the occupants and found a partially empty fifth of sloe gin and some empty beer cans on the floor. The female occupants were obviously intoxicated, and the one who was sitting in the driver's seat with the keys in the ignition was technically in control of the car and therefore "driving." Tragden and Owens made the arrest and now you have two new residents for the weekend, or at least until the out-of-state parents can arrange for bail. The police desk sergeant has no authority to release intoxicated persons on recognizance, because they usually are brought back in before the ink dries on the disposition record.

At the Monday hearing, Judge Orem hears the case along with those of others who could not make bail. He listens intently to their story, noting they are in fresh dresses, clean, and appear younger than their twenty years. Nancy Smith, the more talkative of the two, blames the police. She claims the sloe gin and beer cans belonged to some boys whom they were waiting for at the "Emergency Room," and that they had been abusive to the police officers only after the officers had flashed a spotlight in their eyes. Not only were they not guilty of anything, Nancy asserts, but a conviction of this sort would cause them to be kicked out of their sororities and may hinder their remaining in the local college nursing curriculum. She admits that they took a couple of drinks with their boy friends, but insists that they were minding their own business until the police intruded.

Judge Orem considers the question and calls you to his chambers to ask about their condition and conduct upon being admitted to the jail. You tell the judge the truth, saying that they had not been any trouble, but obviously had been drinking. The judge then asks your opinion as to what the consequences for the two girls' behavior should be. You want to think about the situation carefully before you answer.

INSTRUCTIONS:

Decide on a course of action.

    A. Carefully define the problem.

    B. List all the options or choices you can think of.

    C. Rank these options in order of priority.

    D. Select the option that you think is the best and briefly discuss the probable consequences.

The Court and Child Abuse

As a lawyer you enjoyed private practice. However, after ten years of successful practice, you decided to enter public service and politics. You and your family realized that public service does not have the financial rewards of a private practice, but your ten-year law practice solidified your financial situation. Over the years you made some important personal connections and a good name for yourself. On your first attempt at public service, you were elected county prosecutor. Being a prosecutor was a different kind of law practice; your new job was to convict people in the name of the state instead of defending them. Of the variety of cases you prosecuted, some naturally stirred your interests and working capacity more than others. Because you were a family man, the crime of child abuse was one of the crimes that always seemed to make you press harder. You always attempted to prosecute abusive parents to the full extent of the law and have their children removed to a nonthreatening environment. Trials for this offense always proved to be an emotional experience for you.

Your career as county prosecutor progressed rapidly. Eventually you were appointed a family court judge, a position which again proved to be a different world. You now had to evaluate facts objectively, rather than approaching the case primarily from a prosecutor's or defense lawyer's point of view. Your first case of child abuse as judge was a very difficult experience. The family was very prominent in the community. The police discovered the abuse as a result of a family disturbance call. The abuse had apparently been taking place for a short time, and because of the family's community standing, had been covered up. The abuse seemed to have resulted from marital problems which had led both parents to heavy drinking. During an argument between the couple, their seven-year-old son interrupted them. They had since focused and projected their problems onto the child. The actual physical abuse was usually a belt strap across the back of the young boy. The psychological damage to the youth as a result of his parents' behavior was, of course, impossible to measure.

You are not the county prosecutor or defense attorney now. You are the judge and you must try to do what is best for all concerned, especially the boy. Should you take him out of his home or not? If you do, you will be taking him away from the place he lives and his natural parents. His parents are in the financial position to do a great deal for their son where a government agency could not. More important, the boy does love his parents and seems to want to stay with them. On the other hand, if you do not remove him from the home, he could be subjected to even more severe abuse. Hopefully, the court experience might open the eyes of the parents to their need for professional help in solving their problems and child abuse tendencies, but there is no way to be sure. Do you take the child out of his home or do you let the parents keep custody and hope that the child will not be subjected to further abuse?

INSTRUCTIONS:

Decide on a course of action.

A. Carefully define the problem.
B. List all the options or choices you can think of.
C. Rank these options in order of priority.
D. Select the option that you think is the best and briefly discuss the probable consequences.

The Court and Juvenile Delinquency

You are a juvenile judge. The job is not so easy as some people think. The judicial process in any court is somewhat ambiguous, but the process in a juvenile court is even less defined. With so many options available in the rehabilitation or institutionalization of juveniles, the juvenile judge needs to be particularly careful concerning his or her final decision.

As a juvenile judge, your job is not simply to determine guilt or innocence. Most of the time you have to determine the degree of the juvenile's involvement in a criminal act. Cases come to you informally through complaints and formally through juvenile petitions. You have to interpret and apply not only state criminal laws, but also laws called ''Unruly Acts'' which apply only to juveniles. The philosophy of the juvenile court is to treat and rehabilitate the juvenile offender if at all possible. This philosophy of rehabilitation sometimes results in the same juvenile coming before your court for a second or third appearance. Still, you are reluctant to institutionalize a juvenile except as a last resort.

Today's case presents a difficult problem to you as a juvenile judge. The juvenile is a fifteen-year-old male with whom you are very familiar. He has been in your court several times since he was ten years old. His first encounter with the law was for habitual truancy from school. The problem centered around a lack of parental supervision and concern. The boy began associating with a ''bad'' crowd and his delinquent behavior began to increase. His next encounter with the juvenile justice system was for shoplifting. He was placed on six months' probation. During his probation, he was suspected in several breaking and entering offenses, and it was eventually proved in court that he did participate in one burglary. At age fourteen he was incarcerated in a juvenile corrections center. After seven months, the boy was released on parole. During the next year, he was involved in various liquor violations which, of course, violated his conditions of parole. He spent another four months in the juvenile corrections center.

In the present case this juvenile is accused of the vandalism of a public school. Loss of property resulting from this offense has been estimated at $15,000. The state has requested that the juvenile be tried as an adult. This is one of your toughest decisions as a juvenile judge. Under the law the court must place the child under legal restraints if it decides that to do so is in the best interest of the community. If the juvenile court feels this is warranted, the criminal court must accept the case after a hearing. The case will then go to the grand jury for indictment.

Once the child is released from the juvenile court, he is subject to adult punishment and can incarcerated in the state prison. You feel sure if he is convicted on the $15,000 vandalism charge, he will be sentenced to prison. You wonder if this particular juvenile will ever be able to recover from the stigma of an ''adult'' prison and become a productive citizen. On the other hand, you do have a duty to protect the community from incorrigible juveniles. You must decide whether or not the severity of this case warrants that the child be tried as an adult. Should the community be protected by the legal restraint of this juvenile, or should the boy be protected under the juvenile court in an effort to rehabilitate him?

INSTRUCTIONS:

Decide on a course of action.

   A. Carefully define the problem.
   B. List all the options or choices you can think of.
   C. Rank these options in order of priority.
   D. Select the option that you think is the best and briefly discuss the probable consequences.

Probation or Prison?

You could have been there yourself. Instead, it is Mary Lee Smith, one of your probationers, who is about to stand before the judge in a probation revocation hearing.

When you and your husband split ten years ago, you had two children and eventually had to declare bankruptcy to be able to pay the rent. After seven years working as a secretary at the nearby state juvenile corrections center and taking advantage of the Law Enforcement Education Program at a nearby university, you finished a degree in the Administration of Justice and qualified for an entry level position with the community resources division of the State Department of Corrections. You advanced as the system grew and now, three years later, you are a probation supervisor in Judge Longworth's court.

In a way, Mary Lee is as much a victim as she is an offender. Married at seventeen, she quit high school and moved west with her serviceman husband. By the time she was twenty she had two children and was divorced. With babysitters to pay and skills that would command no more than minimum wage, Mary Lee turned to such income supplements as shoplifting, bad check writing, and occasionally prostitution. Her check passing skills developed rapidly, and it was not long before she had amassed a series of convictions, besides several lesser offenses for petty larceny which were disposed of by the prosecutor's declaration of *nolle prosequi*. To date, Mary Lee has not served a day in prison. Admonition, restitution, suspended sentence, and probation have all been used by Judge Longworth in efforts to rehabilitate Mary Lee. However, Mary Lee's criminal conduct has persisted, as has her inability to stretch her food stamps, welfare payments, and part-time minimum wage employment into a satisfactory existence for herself and her children.

Judge Longworth has called you into his chambers before the hearing. He read your violation report with interest. You pointed out Mary Lee's family obligations and the imminent possibility that the children would have to be placed in foster homes if she is confined. You also pointed out that she has been faithful in making restitution and that she maintains a regular church relationship and a satisfactory home environment for her children. Although your report is fair and accurate, you realize that the judge has sensed your own misgivings and uncertainty concerning Mary Lee.

Judge Longworth looks up from your report and comes directly to the point. "Do you really believe this woman deserves to go back into the community? You certainly seem to have found some redeeming features in her conduct that I don't," he continues. "Unfortunately, it appears to me that the only way she is going to learn to respect other people's property is to be deprived of her own freedom. I think the community is getting pretty tired of this kind of repetitive criminal conduct." With that Judge Longworth looks to you expectantly for an answer.

You are on the spot. You know your answer might put Mary Lee in the penitentiary or give her another chance on probation. The judge will make up his own mind, but you know he values your opinion.

INSTRUCTIONS:

Decide on a course of action.

A. Carefully define the problem.
B. List all the options or choices you can think of.
C. Rank these options in order of priority.
D. Select the option that you think is the best and briefly discuss the probable consequences.

Prescriptions: The Presentence Report

Robert M. Carter

This chapter is targeted directly upon the presentence report—its format and content. It argues the acceptance of several major themes and provides prescriptions which support these basic positions. The assumptions upon which the chapter is constructed are presented first; the prescriptions follow.

A. ASSUMPTIONS

The primary purpose of the presentence report is to provide the sentencing court with relevant and accurate data so it may select the most appropriate sentencing alternative and correctional disposition. Although use of the report for sentencing decision is paramount, its potential use for probation supervision and/or by other agencies within and outside the correctional system should be recognized. These other potential uses may influence determination of the content and format of the report; however, they are subordinate to the primary purpose of providing data which meet judicial needs.

The data requirements for criminal justice decision-making may be best determined by the decision-makers themselves. Therefore, presentence report design, both format and content, should be tailored to meet the needs of the individual criminal justice system. The primary inputs about the report should be made collaboratively by the court and the probation agency. Clearly, data requirements from other criminal justice agencies should be determined and, where possible, incorporated into presentence reports. A singular prescription advocating or portraying "the" model presentence report is inappropriate; to the extent presentence reports are designed carefully by relevant decision-makers, different formats and content are acceptable.

U.S. Department of Justice, January 1978.

Despite a tradition for "longer" rather than "shorter" presentence reports (with neither term well defined here nor anywhere else), there is little evidence that more extensive data are better for decision-makers than less, particularly if less amounts of data are deliberately (rather than traditionally) selected, are relevant and verified. Shorter rather than longer reports are advocated with the caution that a process be established to permit expansion for addressing unusual circumstances about the offense and/or offender.

The 1971 commentary of John Hogarth warrants special attention here:

> There is considerable research evidence suggesting that in human decision-making the capacity of individuals to use information effectively is limited to the use of not more than five or six items of information. In many cases, depending on the kind of information used, the purposes to which it is put, and the capacity of the individual concerned, the limit is much less. Despite this evidence there is a noticeable tendency for presentence reports to become longer. One of the most unfortunate myths in the folklore concerning sentencing, is the notion that the courts should know 'all about the offender.' Quite apart from whether much of the information is likely to be reliable, valid or even relevant to the decision possibilities open to the court, the burden of a mass of data can only result in information-overload and the impairment of the efficiency in which relevant information is handled. This suggests that if probation officers wished to improve the effectiveness of their communications to magistrates they would be advised to shorten their reports.

The standard presentence report should be tailored to meet the needs of individual criminal justice systems and be relatively short. Consideration should be given to including, at a minimum, some commentary in the following data areas:

- Description of the offense
- Prior criminal record
- Personal history
- Evaluation
- Recommendation

The level of detail presented in these data areas—or others if there are additions, modifications or deletions to this list—should be determined by the individual justice system.

Although it is recommended that the standard report address at least the areas above, it should be flexible enough to allow for expansion of both subject areas and the level of detail in each subject area if the circumstances in a particular case so warrant. Guidelines should be developed to spell out the conditions which govern expansion of the standard report to other areas of inquiry or to greater levels of detail.

At a minimum, the preparation of a presentence report is encouraged (a) in every case in which sentencing to confinement for a year or longer is possible and

(b) in all other cases at the discretion of the court. To the extent resources are available, it is recommended that a presentence report be prepared in every case in which the court has a sentencing option, with the kinds of data and levels of detail dependent upon some classification of offense and/or offender, and with explicit operational guidelines for such classification and established by the probation organization and the court.

A probation organization recommendation for or against probation is encouraged, but only if (a) the offender is not seen as a "client" during the presentence investigation and report process (the court is the "client"), (b) the sentencing recommendations are the responsibility of the probation organization and not the individual officer, and (c) the recommendations are measured against probation organization criteria and guidelines so as to enhance consistency and minimize disparities. In making recommendations, the probation organization must understand that the purpose of the report in general and the recommendation in particular is to assist the decision-maker, protect the community, and reduce the probability of continued criminal behavior on the part of the offender.

To the extent that probation is a possible disposition, the presentence investigation and report should provide the sentencing court with data outlining a responsible and achievable plan for probation supervision, identify available resources, and state the recommended terms and/or conditions of probation.

The data contained on the cover sheet (often known as the "face" sheet) of the report should be agreed upon by the court and the probation organization. Though it should be minimal in length, it should include information required for identification or quick reference, i.e., the court docket number, the date of sentencing and the offense. The presentence report should not be written on the cover sheet.

B. PRESCRIPTIONS FOR MULTIPLE PRESENTENCE REPORT FORMATS AND CONTENTS

1. Individual criminal justice jurisdictions should design several gradations or varieties of presentence report formats and content to meet the explicit sentencing needs within the jurisdiction and to respond to varying needs for data about different offenses and/or offenders. These different reports must meet the specific needs of the court and, where possible, the needs of correctional agencies. The court, the probation organization, correctional agencies and other criminal justice organizations should collaborate in the design of presentence report formats.

Commentary

Investigations and reports serve to provide the sentencing court with information and analyses which assist in selecting sentencing dispositions. The information and analyses needed vary by offense/offender and sentencing options available. Investigations and reports may be short if (a) the offense is simple, (b) there are no apparent personal or social complexities, and (c) the sentence cannot exceed one year. In this instance the court may be given merely a "fact sheet," some minimum narrative, and an evaluation. Additional detail may be provided if the offense/

offender is more complicated as, for example, where charges are pending elsewhere, detainers have been filed, violence was part of the offense, etc. Regardless of format, however, there is a requirement for some analysis and evaluation by the probation officer.

There is a need to tailor the investigation and report to the needs of the sentencing court. This tailoring requires the development of a variety of report formats with different formats used for different offenses/offenders or other explicit classification schemes. Because data collected during the investigation are useful to other correctional agencies, collaborative design work to meet other agency data needs is appropriate.

2. The design of multiple presentence report formats and content is primarily a module building exercise. A standard report which includes "x" major areas of interest and "y" levels of detail should be created for the jurisdiction. This standard report should be used "most" of the time. For a variety of explicit reasons (most likely centering upon unusual offense, offender or circumstances surrounding the case), additional areas of interest or levels of detail may be specified for inclusion in an expanded report.

Commentary

Upon finding that a standard report is inadequate to meet decision-makers' needs, a jurisdiction should have two basic options for improving the report. The first option is to utilize another "standard" report which automatically adds areas of interest and/or levels of detail. Thus, a jurisdiction might have two or more standard reports with the "shorter" one used most of the time and guidelines describing those circumstances when the "longer" presentence report should be utilized. The second option simply adds special areas of interest or increases the level of detail on an ad hoc basis following a discussion of the case between the probation organization and the sentencing court.

Whether two or more reports are utilized in the jurisdiction or additional modules are added by the court/probation organization on a case-by-case basis, it is essential that guidelines be established for preparation of reports other than the basic or standard model.

3. In designing multiple presentence report formats, criminal justice jurisdictions should determine: (a) the general areas of information seen as essential about the offense and offender *and* (b) the amount of detail required in each of those areas. Thus, there is a requirement for identifying subject areas of interest and the levels of detail about those subject areas.

Commentary

The multiple presentence report formats and content designed by a jurisdiction may be constructed of modules, each one of which focuses upon specific areas of information. Eighteen possible areas of information, or modules, which may be relevant to judicial and correctional decision-making are:

- Legal Chronology and Related Data
- Offense
- Prior Record
- Personal History
- Physical Environment (home and neighborhood)
- Personal Environment
- Education and Training
- Religious Involvement
- Interests and Leisure Time Activities
- Physical Health and History
- Mental Health and History
- Employment and Employment History
- Military Service
- Financial Status: Assets and Liabilities
- Resources Available
- Summary
- Evaluation and Prognosis
- Treatment Plan and Recommendation

This list is to be viewed only as illustrative. The list may be expanded or contracted readily by separating or joining together areas of information: for example, "treatment plan and recommendation," now combined, could be separated into discrete areas of information; conversely, "physical and mental health" could become a broader, more inclusive area of information simply by combining the two categories. It also may be desirable to add areas of information which are not suggested at all in the above listing or to delete one or more of those suggested as not relevant to requirements and needs in a particular jurisdiction. Then too, the order and sequence of these eighteen areas of information are to be viewed as illustrative. Each one of the eighteen broad subject areas contains a list of "bits of information" which may be useful to the decision-maker. . . .

The modular construction process suggests that the designers of presentence report formats and content first identify the broad subject areas of interest (from this list of eighteen possibilities or some other list). The designers should then select from the chosen subject areas explicit items of information which seem particularly relevant to decision-making in the jurisdiction. Thus, a two-step process is recommended: determination of those broad areas which are of particular interest in a jurisdiction and then selection of specific bits of data to flesh out the skeleton. The areas of interest become the paragraph or topical headings in the report; the specific data become the content.

It is essential to recognize that neither the eighteen subject areas nor the lists of data which comprise each of them are seen as exhaustive. The headings and items of data are meant to be illustrative of the two-step process.

4. Although presentence reports are tailored to meet the needs of the individual criminal justice jurisdiction, they normally should include some comment about the following areas:

- Description of the Offense
- Prior Criminal Record
- Personal History
- Evaluation
- Recommendation

The level of detail about these five areas—and/or others if there are additions, modifications, or deletions to the list—should be determined by the individual criminal justice jurisdiction and should vary according to the offense and/or offender.

Commentary

Several studies on judicial and correctional decision-making have indicated that the current offense, the prior criminal record and personal history are important to the probation officer's selection of a recommendation for sentencing and to the court's selection of the sentence. The evaluation represents the probation officer's assessment of those factors which resulted in the offender's appearance before the court for sentencing, the resources which will be required to assist the offender to avoid further conflict with the law, and estimates of the probability of further law violations and of the risk to community safety should probation be granted.

A recommendation that the offender be placed on probation should include the proposed conditions of probation and a plan of supervision. The resources available and required should be identified.

5. The narrative portion of the presentence report should be arranged topically.

Commentary

Regardless of format, presentence reports should be arranged topically. Such arrangement provides continuity and clarity and facilitates understanding and utilization by court and probation personnel. Consistency in topical arrangement saves organizational resources and insures completeness.

6. The sentencing court, in collaboration with the probation organization, should set guidelines specifying which presentence report format is to be utilized in particular types of cases.

Commentary

The policies which emerge from the collaborative determination of case-format requirements should be in writing and reviewed regularly. As a basic principle, they should insure that enough data are collected and analyzed so that the most appropriate sentencing alternative may be selected to protect the community and serve the needs of the offender.

7. At the discretion of the probation organization or the direction of the court, the presentence report should be expanded to address unusual circumstances surrounding the offense, the offender or community reaction and concern.

Commentary

The requirement for flexibility mandates that reports be expanded when it appears that they cannot otherwise provide an accurate portrayal of the offense/ offender, unusual circumstances in the case or community concern. The option to expand should lie both with the probation organization at its discretion and the court at its direction.

8. The sentencing court, in collaboration with the probation organization, should set guidelines specifying the conditions or circumstances which warrant expansion of a presentence report.

Commentary

In order to promote consistency within the organization, the court and the probation organization collaboratively should establish general criteria for expansion of reports. These criteria should make constant discussion of format changes unnecessary. The guidelines should be in writing and should be reviewed regularly. However, these guidelines should not prohibit discussions of report format adjustments in particular cases.

9. Data presented in the presentence report should be verified; unverified information should be identified as such.

Commentary

It is essential that verified and unsubstantiated data be identified in presentence reports. Too great a risk is presented to the community, the probation organization and the offender when unverified data are commingled with verified data. Rumors, allegations, second-hand and unverified data, if included at all in reports, must be clearly identified as such.

Some of the data collected by the probation organization will be "secondary" data—developed originally by some other organization. There must be attempts to verify the accuracy of secondary data and equal efforts to insure that primary data—that collected by the organization itself—are accurate. Sources and procedures which tend to yield erroneous data should be eliminated. Written policies and guidelines and supervision will reduce many errors.

10. Presentence reports should contain those data which are relevant to judicial dispositional decision-making. "Nice to know" information should not be included in presentence reports. The information provided the court

both in terms of format and detail should be tailored to meet the sentencing alternatives available.

Commentary

Regardless of report format, the data in the presentence report must be of a "need to know" variety. The determination of "need to know" data may best be made by the court in collaboration with the probation organization. Long reports with irrelevant data are not utilized; they waste valuable resources in preparation and review. The amount of data "needed" may vary by the sentencing alternatives available.

The Cover Sheet

11. One standardized cover sheet (or face sheet) should be designed by the criminal justice jurisdiction. It should contain a minimum amount of data— primarily information for identification or quick reference such as docket number, offense and date of sentencing. The data included should be agreed upon by the court and the probation organization. The cover sheet is not a substitute for the presentence report; cover sheet data generally should not be repeated in the report itself.

Commentary

The cover sheet, which should be limited to one page, is an excellent location for supplemental data such as social security number, law enforcement agency identification numbers, date of birth, etc. These identification data insure that case files, information and persons are properly matched. The cover sheet should be factual and complete as of the date of its submission to the court.

In developing a cover sheet, the agency should consider data processing potential in the jurisdiction and design the sheet to facilitate the removal of data for computer-based operations.

12. The probation officer should make a recommendation for or against probation to the court in every case. The recommendation should be in accord with general probation organization guidelines and policy.

Commentary

The probation officer, through the presentence investigation and report process, should be able to offer some particularly useful insights about the various sentencing alternatives as they relate to community safety, the probability of continuing criminal behavior, and offender needs and available resources. Accordingly, the officer should make a recommendation to the court regarding the granting or denial of probation. The recommendation should be consistent with recommendations made in similar cases and be in accord with general probation organization guidelines. Disparities in recommendations contribute to disparities in sentencing. Recommendations that differ substantially from organizational policy should be fully justified and reviewed with supervisors.

13. The probation organization guidelines for presentence report recommendations should discourage imprisonment and encourage probation as the recommended disposition providing that community safety is not endangered, that supervision will enhance community protection, and that the offender is in need of correctional programming which can be provided most effectively in the community.

Commentary

Probation is an appropriate disposition providing that the safety of the community is not endangered and that programs available in the community can meet identified needs of the offender. Judgments about these factors must evolve from presentence investigations and reports and should be expressed in the recommendation.

14. When the probation organization recommends to the sentencing court that probation be granted a convicted offender, it should be with the understanding that probation is a sentencing disposition which places an offender in the community under supervision.

Commentary

The purpose of probation supervision is to protect the community and reduce the probability of continued criminal behavior on the part of the probationer. Supervision must provide effective monitoring of and service to probationers, but public safety is paramount. The types and intensities of supervision to provide community protection should be tailored as should the utilization of community resources to meet probationer needs.

15. In making a recommendation for or against probation, the probation organization should not be influenced by plea or sentence bargaining commitments.

Commentary

The presentence report should contain an objective assessment and impartial evaluation of the offender; the recommendation for or against probation should reflect the best professional judgment of probation personnel. The evaluation and recommendation should not be constrained by formal or informal agreements entered into by other personnel in the criminal justice system relating to plea or sentence bargaining. To allow such agreements to influence the report is to corrupt the objective fact-finding purpose of presentence activity.

The Conditions of Probation

16. The conditions of probation should be definite, few in number, realistic, and phrased in positive rather than negative terms. The conditions are neither vague nor ambiguous.

Commentary

The conditions of probation are the standards for probationer behavior in the community. These standards must be clear, positive, equitable, realistic and few in number. To expect compliance with vague, tenuous and unrealistic conditions is itself unrealistic and jeopardizes the possibility of successful probationer adjustment. The probationer has a right to know what is expected of him.

The conditions of probation should be reviewed with all staff members so there is consistency in application and equity for all probationers. Conditions of probation should be developed in collaboration with the court.

17. As part of a presentence report recommendation for probation, the probation officer should identify the need for special conditions of probation, if any, and recommend that these special conditions be appended to the conditions of probation.

Commentary

In addition to those general conditions of probation which are applicable to all probationers, possible special conditions should be identified during the presentence investigation and recommended to the court. If it appears that these additional conditions will enhance public safety or increase the probability of a successful community adjustment, they should be appended by the court to the general conditions. Special conditions should be tailored to individual probationers.

Written policies about special conditions should be developed collaboratively by the probation organization and the court and should be reviewed regularly.

A Plan for Probation Supervision

18. A plan for supervision of individuals selected for probation should be developed during the presentence investigation and included as part of the presentence report.

Commentary

The appropriate time to develop a plan for a possible period of probation is during the presentence investigation. Should probation be granted, a plan will be available on the first day of supervision. The plan, which should include such basic considerations as employment, residence, education, and so on, should be developed with the defendant during the investigation. The plan must be realistic in that the goals set with the probationer are attainable and the resources required are available or are capable of being developed. The probation plan identifies that which should be done by stating probation objectives; it also identifies the means for achievement of objectives. Plans help eliminate ad hoc supervision practice.

19. During the presentence investigation, special attention should be given to seeking innovative alternatives to traditional sentencing dispositions of probation, jail or imprisonment. Attention also should be directed to finding or

generating resources which permit individualized probation supervision programs to be utilized if probation is ordered by the sentencing court.

Commentary

The traditional dispositions in the adult courts are probation, confinement in a local facility or confinement in a state correctional institution or a combination of these. It is important to seek other alternatives which will permit the tailoring of a court disposition to the protection of the community and the needs of the offender. The appropriate time to search for alternatives is during the presentence investigation; innovation and creativity are to be encouraged. The use of alternatives such as halfway houses, detoxification centers, civil addict commitment programs, self-help groups, public service projects and/or restitution to victims and reparation to the general public may be appropriate.

C. SUMMARY

This chapter adopts the position that the primary purpose of the presentence report is to provide the sentencing court with relevant and accurate data so the the court may select the most appropriate sentencing alternative considering both community safety and a reduction in the probability of continued criminal behavior on the part of the convicted offender. Building upon this premise, the data required to make decisions should be identified by the decision-maker—the court—in collaboration with its investigative arm, the probation organization, and other criminal justice agencies, primarily correctional. Inasmuch as different jurisdictions may have different criteria for decision-making, it is appropriate for different presentence report designs to be utilized. However, all designs should be a conscious and deliberate response to the identification of data requirements for decision-making.

Jurisdictions designing presentence reports are encouraged to utilize a modular approach and to follow a two-step process: (a) identification of broad subject areas of information and (b) determination of the level of detail required within those broad subject areas. . . .

It is recommended that each jurisdiction design a standard report and establish guidelines which allow for expansion of that report when circumstances so dictate. Expansion should entail either use of a more extensive report (in subject areas and/or levels of detail) or addition of modules on an ad hoc basis after consultation between the court and probation organization. It is urged that the standard report be "short" and capable of being expanded rather than "long" and capable of being reduced.

Further, to the extent resources are or can be made available, a presentence report on all convicted offenders is recommended. Varying presentence report designs should be utilized for different types of offenses and/or offenders, as predetermined by collaborative efforts within the criminal justice community. Finally, it is strongly suggested that the cover sheet contain primarily reference or identification data and that its length and content be minimal rather than extensive and all-inclusive.

Prescriptions: The Presentence Environment

Robert M. Carter

The presentence investigation and subsequent preparation of a presentence report are not activities conducted in isolation from a larger probation-corrections-criminal justice environment. Presentence activities are impacted by a variety of forces in this nonpresentence environment including societal changes, divergent and sometimes transient philosophies about criminal justice in general and corrections in particular, political and economic considerations, legal decisions, organizational, administrative, management and decision-making arrangements, and the like. These many forces, not always visible, often impact upon presentence activities of probation organizations in subtle, but significant ways.

The purpose of this chapter is to provide a limited number of general prescriptions not directly related to the content and format of the presentence report. Grouped more or less homogeneously, these prescriptions are a direct response to specific concerns surfaced by some correctional administrators. . . . It is certainly true that many of these prescriptions are "obvious," such as the need to have the probation organization free from political influence and to have adequate resources. It is equally true that the regularity with which these subjects were surfaced by administrators suggest some real constraints in practice. These prescriptions were designed to be responsive to expressed concerns of probation administrators; some may be controversial, others may be decided by judicial decisions, but all are relevant because presentence practice may be significantly impacted by their adoption or rejection.

Although not explicitly attributed, some of these prescriptions were drawn from the National Advisory Commission on Criminal Justice Standards and Goals, while others were selected from draft standards prepared for the Commission on Accreditation for Corrections. Finally, some were extracted from standard operating procedures (SOP's) provided by correctional administrators. . . .

U.S. Department of Justice, January 1978.

PURPOSE OF THE PRESENTENCE REPORT

20. The primary purpose of the presentence report should be to provide the sentencing court with relevant and accurate data in a timely fashion so that it may select the most appropriate sentencing alternative.

Commentary

Although use of the report for the sentencing decision is paramount, its potential use by other agencies in the correctional system should be recognized. These other potential uses may be factors in determining the content and format of the report; but the primary purpose of meeting judicial sentencing needs is not subordinated to them.

CASES REQUIRING PRESENTENCE REPORTS

21. A presentence report should be prepared by the probation organization and presented to the court in every case in which there is a potential sentencing disposition involving incarceration for one year or longer.

Commentary

The loss of freedom through a sentence of confinement is a most severe sanction. To insure that the decision to select the confinement alternative is most appropriate, it is essential that the sentencing court have accurate, complete and relevant data in all cases in which sentences in excess of one year are possible. The one-year time frame is arbitrary: a thirty-day sentence to confinement is significant. As resources become available, presentence reports should be prepared in other cases in which confinement is an alternative. The presentence report may become both a legal record and a portrait of the offender.

22. For cases other than those involving incarceration, the court should have discretion to request that the probation organization prepare and present a presentence report to the court.

Commentary

It is essential that the court have the authority to order a presentence investigation and report in any case if it will enhance the selection of that sentence which best serves to protect the community and meet the needs of the offender.

RESOURCES

23. All sentencing courts should be provided with probation resources which permit accomplishment of presentence investigations and written reports.

Commentary

Sentencing courts must have probation resources which permit presentence investigations and written reports. These investigations provide relevant and accurate information for the critical sentencing decisions which can so significantly impact upon the community and the offender.

24. An adequate number of qualified probation staff or proportion of staff time should be assigned to the presentence function.

Commentary

Regardless of how the probation organization is structured to carry out the investigation function, the personnel assigned to that function must be adequate in number and qualified by ability, interest and training. "Adequate" staff is defined in terms of productivity standards developed by the probation organization. Investigations and reports should be assigned equitably in the interest of fairness, maintenance of morale, productivity and quality of work. Continuous training and supervision will insure high performance in the investigation function.

25. Adequate support staff and related resources should be allocated to the presentence function.

Commentary

Sufficient auxiliary staff—clerks, typists, volunteers, paraprofessionals—must be available to support the investigation and report functions. "Adequate" is defined in terms of performance standards rather than precise numbers. Equipment such as typewriters and dictating equipment and related supplies must also be available to support the functions.

26. The probation organization should have a space management program which insures adequate facilities for all of its operations.

Commentary

The purpose of the space management program is to enhance delivery of services to the courts and probationers. An annual review of space requirements should consider manpower, equipment, functions, adequacy of current space, location, privacy, safety and other related matters. Particular attention should be given to enhancing communication between and among probation staff, subjects of presentence investigations, probationers, and others.

27. The facilities and the space management program of the probation organization should insure that presentence activities are conducted at locations that are readily accessible to the subjects of these activities.

Commentary

The location of space for presentence activities may be at sites other than in courthouses and similar public facilities. Convenience, access to transportation, community orientation and a general enhancing of operations are significant considerations.

28. Probation personnel should be reimbursed for all necessary expenses incurred in the performance of their duties.

Commentary

Probation personnel must be reimbursed for their actual and necessary expenses incurred in the line of duty. The budget process at the beginning of the year and supervision of the budget during the year should insure that adequate funds are available.

ORGANIZATION AND ADMINISTRATION

29. The operations of the probation organization should be free from improper political influence.

Commentary

Improper political influence from within or outside the organization must not be allowed to impact upon organizational decision-making relating to either probation personnel or offenders/probationers. Political intrigue will do irreparable damage to the agency by eroding public confidence and, further, will prohibit the development of a professional probation organization.

30. Responsibilities and functions of the probation organization should be specified by statute, rules of the court, the parent correctional agency or, in their absence, by the organization itself.

Commentary

A probation organization may best achieve its goals and objectives when responsibilities and functions are articulated clearly either by its parent agency or by statute. Uncertain or vague responsibilities and functions will hinder both individual and organizational effectiveness and result in a loss of understanding and support from criminal justice and nonjustice agencies and the general public. Sound management principles such as management by objectives cannot be initiated if the objectives are tenuous and ill defined.

31. The authority and responsibilities of the administrator of the probation organization should be specified by statute, rules of the court, the parent correctional agency or, in their absence, by the organization itself.

Commentary

Just as it is essential that probation organization functions and responsibilities are clearly defined, so too is it essential that the authority of the administrator and the responsibilities given him are defined. Leadership of the probation organization cannot evolve or be maintained if the roles and responsibilities of the administrator are unclear. A clear definition of roles and responsibilities also provides guidance for probation operations and potential for evaluation of performance.

32. The administrator of the probation organization ultimately should be held responsible for all that his organization does or fails to do. This responsibility cannot be delegated to subordinates.

Commentary

The administrator alone is responsible for that which his organization does or fails to do. He meets this challenge by organizing his agency, providing direction and supervision, policy determination and planning, control and inspection, and development of personnel. He must manage his resources to meet goals and objectives.

GOALS AND OBJECTIVES

33. The administrator of the probation organization should be responsible for coordinating the development and formulating the goals of the organization, establishing policies and priorities related to them, and translating the goals into measurable objectives for accomplishment by probation staff.

Commentary

A basic requirement of the probation administrator is the balancing of organizational goals and objectives with the resources available. There are seldom surplus resources available (personnel, time, dollars, etc.). To use resources wisely, the administrator must translate broad organizational goals into more specific objectives which are then prioritized for accomplishment by staff. Without prioritized goals and objectives, the organization will be without focus, continuity or consistency. Articulation of priorities not only serves the organization, but also provides "external" benefits by informing criminal justice and nonjustice agencies and the public of probation goals and objectives. It is essential that the administration obtain inputs about goals, objectives and techniques for achieving them from his staff, the courts, the criminal justice agencies, and the community.

34. All operations of the probation organization should be assessed for results by the administrator of the organization or his designated representatives. Assessments should be done through inspections and reviews of policies, procedures and data.

Commentary

Timely and periodic assessment of the performance of the organization assures the administrator that all standards (organizational, management, programmatic, etc.) are being applied and met. This internal administrative assessment process should exist apart from any external or ongoing audit conducted by other agencies.

35. Assignments and duties in the probation organization should carry with them the commensurate authority to fulfill the responsibilities. Persons in the probation organization to whom authority is delegated should be held accountable both for the use made of it and for the failure to use it.

Commentary

Assignments and duties cannot be achieved and fulfilled and personnel cannot be held accountable for their accomplishment unless they are authorized to use and manage resources of the probation organization. Authority and responsibility are inseparable in practice. Authority is delegated by the probation administrator to his subordinates so that organizational objectives may be accomplished. This authority must neither be abused nor interpreted to extend beyond that which is required by the specific assignment. Conversely, the failure to use authority and the subsequent failure to achieve organizational objectives cannot be condoned.

36. Tasks, similar or related in purpose, process, method, geographic location or clientele, should be grouped together in the probation organization in one or more units under the control of one person.

Commentary

To facilitate the assignment and accomplishment of tasks, the tasks should be divided according to time, place of performance and level of authority needed in their accomplishment. A probation organization will have diverse goals and objectives. Efficiency and effective utilization of resources require that similar duties or tasks be consolidated under the control of one person.

37. Specialized units should be created in the probation organization only when overall capability would be increased significantly.

Commentary

It is not practical to create a specialized unit in the probation organization for every conceivable function. Indeed, too much specialization may result in indifference to overall organizational goals and objectives. Specialized units should be created only if the management of resources and accomplishment of objectives would be enhanced. Specialized units must be needed, contribute to objectives, and assist in meeting established priorities. The continued existence of specialized units should be assessed regularly and terminated when the units no longer contribute to goals and objectives.

38. The span of control of a supervisor in the probation organization should be large enough to provide cost effective supervision; however, it should not be so large that the supervisor cannot manage the units or personnel under his direct control.

Commentary

Depending in large measure upon the size of the probation organization and the responsibilities assigned to it, it may be necessary to add supervisors to the organization to insure that all objectives are being met effectively and efficiently.

39. Effective supervision should be provided for every member of the probation organization and for every function or activity.

Commentary

To insure that agency objectives are being met, it is essential that every individual, function and activity in the organization be supervised. Organizations neither manage nor administer themselves.

40. The probation organization should have legal counsel available.

Commentary

The probation organization operates within a legal framework. Legal staff must be available for timely consultation on a wide range of issues to insure that the public, the agency and the probationer are afforded the legal protection to which they are entitled. It is not essential that counsel be a staff member of the organization.

41. The probation organization should have a public information/relations program which includes the development and distribution of information about the department, its philosophy and operations.

Commentary

The probation organization will benefit from an enlightened public and informed agencies within and outside the criminal justice system. The organization should establish an information program which insures that the probation organization and its goals and objectives are known. The program should address generalized information requirements and should provide for specific commentary about newsworthy incidents. The program should be proactive and geared to all segments of the community from school groups to senior citizens. The use of probation organization personnel to give speeches, write reports, make media presentations, etc. should be encouraged. Opportunities to inform and educate other agencies and the public should be welcomed.

THE MANAGEMENT OF PRESENTENCE ACTIVITIES

42. The administrator of the probation organization should be responsible for the organization and management of the investigation and reporting functions so as to effectively and efficiently provide presentence services to the court.

Commentary

The investigation function is dependent upon the organization and system established to perform it. Investigations and reports comprise a significant amount of total probation activity. Where demands for investigations are great, it may be more efficient and effective to provide for a substructure within the organization with a separate responsibility for the function. When investigation requirements are low, consolidation of the investigation and supervision functions may be practical. In either case, responsibility for the investigation function should be assigned to a member of the staff at the administrative level. A logical, orderly and expeditious work flow from assignment of a requirement for an investigation to completion and delivery of the report to the court is required.

43. The administrator of the probation organization should insure that appropriate priority is assigned to the timely completion of presentence investigations and reports with minimal adverse effect upon the delivery of other probation services.

Commentary

The expeditious completion of presentence investigations and reports is a high priority. Inordinate periods of detention for offenders awaiting sentence are not in the best interests of justice. Special attention must be given to meeting court scheduled sentencing dates while also meeting other probation requirements. Other functions, supervision, for example, cannot be neglected. Probation management must schedule completion dates for reports so as to organize the total workload most effectively. A presentence investigation and report preparation should not exceed three weeks in general or two weeks for offenders in custody. These time frames, however, must always consider the nature of the offense, complexity of the offender's circumstances, possible dispositions, availability of prior reports and the fact that the reports must be delivered to the court in time for review and analysis.

44. The probation organization, not the individual probation officer, should be held accountable for the conduct of presentence investigations, preparation of reports, and selection of sentencing recommendations for the court. Written guidelines should be provided the probation staff for the conduct of presentence investigations, preparation of reports, and selection of sentencing recommendations for the court. A clear policy indicating who signs the presentence report should be articulated.

Commentary

Although individual probation officers conduct investigations, prepare reports and select sentencing recommendations, they do so in the name of the probation organization. As such, the officers must operate within general guidelines and policies of the organization. It is essential that the quality of investigations and reports be high and that disparities in recommendations be minimal. Written guidelines should be developed in collaboration with the court and reviewed regularly.

45. The conduct of presentence investigations, report preparation and selection of sentencing recommendations for the court should be subject to ongoing supervision and review by the administrator of the probation organization.

Commentary

As is the case with every probation function, the administrator of the probation organization or his delegated representative must provide supervision and review of operations. The fact that clearly defined policies exist in the organization does not lessen the requirement for supervision. Supervision insures quality control of the probation process.

46. The probation organization should insure that effective coordination and communication exist with agencies in the criminal justice system and with other public and private agencies and organizations which can impact upon the organization's delivery of services to the court and to probationers. These agencies and organizations include but are not limited to labor unions, churches, schools, civic groups, social service agencies, and employment services.

Commentary

Clearly, the probation organization does not operate within a vacuum; rather, it is closely tied to other justice and nonjustice agencies and the community. The delivery of services is closely related to the understanding and good will of other agencies. Communication networks must therefore be established with them. It is important that organizational linkages include criminal justice councils, planning units, community councils and the like.

47. In those cases where confinement of the adjudicated offender or special community treatment is ordered, probation organization procedures should insure the timely transmittal of presentence report data to the institution or community treatment agency.

Commentary

In those instances in which the offender is sentenced to confinement or community treatment is ordered, presentence materials should be provided to the receiving institution to assist in its classification process. Written guidelines, developed in collaboration with agencies receiving committed offenders, should be available and should cover such matters as method and timing of transmittal of documents.

TIMING FOR INVESTIGATIONS AND REPORTS

48. A presentence (or predisposition) investigation should not be conducted nor a presentence report prepared until the defendant has been adjudicated guilty of an offense unless the three following conditions exist: (1) the defendant, on advice of counsel, has consented to allow the investigation to proceed before adjudication; (2) the defendant is incarcerated pending trial; and (3) adequate precautions are taken to assure that information disclosed during the presentence investigation does not come to the attention of the prosecution, the court or the jury prior to adjudication.

Commentary

The conduct of a presentence investigation and completion of a report prior to adjudication of the charges appear to be unnecessary. At an absolute minimum, however, the conditions of consent, confinement and adequate precautions against disclosure must be met prior to preadjudication investigations and reports. This preadjudication process should be used only under exceptional circumstances, for findings of not guilty mean a waste of resources; compromise of information is always possible; and other alternatives exist for removing a defendant from preadjudication confinement.

49. The probation organization should be given sufficient time by the court to conduct an adequate presentence investigation and prepare an appropriate report.

Commentary

If presentence reports are to provide relevant and verified data to the courts to assist in judicial decision-making, it is essential that adequate time be available for the investigation and report writing function. Although precise time frames cannot be identified, a target of three weeks for nonconfined offenders appears reasonable; a maximum of two weeks may be appropriate for offenders in custody. In setting time frames, consideration must be given to the type and format of the report, the nature of the offense, sentencing options available to the courts, etc. Time frames for investigations and reports should be developed in collaboration with the courts.

50. The presentence report should be submitted to the court for review and evaluation well in advance of the date set for sentencing. The probation officer and/or an appropriate supervisor should be available to discuss the report with the sentencing judge in chambers.

Commentary

The presentence report must be delivered to the court in sufficient time for review and evaluation. Preparation of quality reports is irrelevant if the court does not have sufficient time to read and assess the document and perhaps discuss it with probation staff. A minimum of two full days is seen as essential for the court's review, but this generalized time frame must be adjusted to judicial schedules and work-loads. The probation officer and/or his supervisor should be available to discuss the report with the sentencing judge. The purposes of such a meeting include insuring that the report is complete and accurate and that the court understands fully the data presented.

THE USE OF NONPROFESSIONALS

51. The probation organization should use staff other than probation officers to collect basic, factual information during the presentence investigation, thus freeing the officers from routine investigative functions and permitting them to use their skills more appropriately.

Commentary

Some of the factual data required in an investigation and for the presentence report may be collected by nonprofessional staff, thus freeing the probation officer to use his skills in such nonroutine matters as interpretation of data and development of a probation plan. Examples of data which may be collected readily by nonprofessionals are school records, prior employment verification, etc.

52. Probation officers should be released from routine clerical and rec-ordkeeping duties through the assignment of clerical personnel, paraprofessionals and volunteers.

Commentary

There are many tasks which may be completed by other than professional personnel. Probation officers should be relieved from routine functions in order that they may utilize their particular skills most effectively. The freeing of professional personnel from nonprofessional functions conserves resources, increases job satis-faction and overall productivity. Training must be made available to nonprofessionals to insure that newly acquired duties can be accomplished; super-vision is required to insure that they are accomplished.

CONFIDENTIALITY

53. Sentencing courts should have procedures to inform the defendant of the basis for the sentence imposed and afford him the opportunity to challenge it. These procedures insure that the defendant and counsel are, at a minimum, advised generally of the factual contents of the report.

Commentary

Fairness to the defendant dictates that he be advised of the basis for the sentence imposed and be given an opportunity to challenge the sentence. Since the court's decision-making at least in part will be influenced by the contents of the presentence report, the court should be prepared to summarize the factual contents of the report. The court should also consider summarizing the evaluation and recommendation of the probation officer. The identity of persons providing data about the offender to the probation organization should be protected.

54. Sentencing courts should have the discretionary power to permit inspection of the presentence report by the defendant and his counsel, the prosecution, and others who have a legitimate and proper interest in its contents.

Commentary

Examination of the presentence report should be permitted by the court in those instances where there is a conflict about factual data and where fairness to the defendant warrants full disclosure. Even here, particular attention must be given to the problem of identification of sources of data. The probation organization and the courts should collaboratively establish policy about disclosure of sources of data. The policy should be in writing and reviewed regularly.

CASE RECORDS

55. The probation organization should have written policies and procedures concerning case record management.

Commentary

Case records play an important role in planning, implementing and evaluating programs in the probation organization. The orderly recording, management and maintenance of data increase the efficiency and effectiveness of service delivery to the courts and probationers. Case records are a major component of the administration and delivery of services. These records are essential for sound decision-making and serve as the memory system of the organization. There must be policies to control the establishment, utilization, content, privacy, security, preservation, and timely destruction of case records.

56. The probation organization should maintain a single master index system identifying active, inactive, transferred and destroyed case records.

Commentary

A single master index identifying all case records is an important management tool. It should be centrally located for easy accessibility and include identification data such as name, date of birth, case number, disposition of file if not available, etc. For probation organizations with branch offices, a separate file for active branch office cases is appropriate.

57. The probation organization should insure that the contents of case records are appropriately separated and identified according to an established format.

Commentary

The standardization of case files leads to efficiency and effectiveness. A logical sequence for filing would be intake data, legal documents, the presentence report, and supervision history. Case records management is improved by training professional and clerical personnel.

58. The confidentiality of presentence reports and case records should be safeguarded from unauthorized and improper disclosure. Written procedures should be developed to prevent unauthorized disclosure.

Commentary

The issue of confidentiality extends beyond the courtroom: it must permeate the entire investigation and report process from receipt of the case for investigation through final destruction of documents. Information about cases should not be discussed openly and files and records should not be left unattended or be given to persons who do not have a proper and legitimate interest in the case. Concern and action to prevent compromise of information is essential.

59. The probation organization should have policies concerning the security of, accessibility to, and destruction of case records.

Commentary

Case records must be located so that they are accessible to the staff members who use them. Records must be safeguarded from unauthorized disclosure, locked when not under supervision to prevent unauthorized access. A clear written policy relating to destruction of case records should be established in collaboration with the courts.

60. The probation organization should insure that the materials and equipment utilized for the maintenance of case records are efficient and economical.

Commentary

The costs of processing and storing probation records are such that controls are required. Purchase of equipment or supplies for processing and storage should be related to anticipated needs; an equipment inventory should be maintained. Files must be protected against fire, theft, water damage, etc. The location of files should facilitate work flow.

STANDARD OPERATING PROCEDURES

61. The administrator of the probation organization should be responsible for the development and maintenance of an administrative manual or "standard operating procedure." The manual should be available to all staff and include the rules, regulations, policies and procedures which govern (a) the conduct of probation operations and (b) staff activities and behavior.

Commentary

The probation organization should have a single source for its established policies and procedures; it must be available to all personnel to facilitate consistency in organizational operations. The efficient management of resources is enhanced when all personnel understand how operations are to be conducted and have available to them expectations of personal behavior and definitions of organizational activities. The manual should be divided into at least two parts: (a) conduct of operations (Examples: case recording, report writing, presentence activities) and (b) staff behavior (Examples: client relations, media contacts, employee benefits). The manual should leave little doubt as to what is expected in the organization, although some considerable individual discretion must be allowed. The manual is also useful in explaining the probation organization to other public and private organizations.

62. All policies and procedures of the probation organization should be written and be reviewed at least annually, or more frequently, as appropriate.

Commentary

The functions and roles of the probation organization do not remain static. Thus, all policies and procedures should be reviewed at least annually to insure that the organization is meeting its goals and objectives efficiently and effectively, and that resources are being utilized properly. Changes in policies and procedures should be reflected in the administrative manual for all personnel must have access to current requirements. The use of a looseleaf binder will facilitate the maintenance of an up-to-date policies and procedures file.

63. Policies and procedures of the probation organization should be known by employees and controls should be established to insure compliance.

Commentary

Rules and regulations, policies and procedures, in part developed by staff and always known to them through staff meetings, training, and administrative manuals, must be followed. Failure to comply with organizational policy and regulation may reasonably be expected to result in adverse consequences to the organization and the individual. Compliance provides consistency and equity; supervision is essential.

A CODE OF ETHICS

64. The probation organization should have a code of ethics developed by those personnel who are subject to its provisions.

Commentary

A code of ethics, serving to guide the professional and personal behavior of probation organization personnel, should be stated in a positive manner and be general in nature. The code should stress commitment to the community, the public service, the criminal justice system and the dignity of individuals. It should emphasize also such personal characteristics as integrity, objectivity, and professionalism.

There is a difference between organizational policies and procedures and a code of ethics. For example, organizational policy appropriately would prohibit the accepting of a gift or gratuity or engaging in personal business transactions with a probationer or his immediate family; a code of ethics would address the larger concern of conflict of interest generally.

SUMMARY

Reviewers of these prescriptions should note that they are presented in response to specific concerns raised by some probation administrators in the course of the presentence activity survey described earlier. As such, they should not be considered as the complete list of prescriptions impacting upon presentence activity. Probation administrators and organizations seeking more complete prescriptions and standards for probation in general and presentence activity in particular should closely follow the development of total probation standards by the Commission on Accreditation for Corrections.

The prescriptions in this chapter are deliberately general in nature, for it is certain that there are requirements for modification to meet specific probation organization needs. Clearly, the administrative location of the probation organization within the criminal justice system, the types of services required by legislation and policy, organization, size, traditions and other concerns will influence the tailoring of these broad prescriptions to meet explicit needs. But while modification of general prescriptions to meet specific organizational needs is completely appropriate, the acceptance or rejection of these and/or similar standards will impact significantly upon the presentence investigation and report.

Selected Bibliography

BARON, ROGER, and FEENEY, FLOYD. *Juvenile Diversion Through Family Counseling*, U.S. Department of Justice, February, 1976.

BARTON, WILLIAM H. "Discretionary Decision-Making in Juvenile Justice." *Crime and Delinquency*, 22(1976):470–480.

BLOOM, MURRAY. "Conciliation Court: Crisis Intervention in Domestic Violence." *Crime Prevention Review*, 6(1978):19–24.

CLEAR, TODD R.; HEWITT, JOHN D.; and REGOLI, ROBERT M. "Discretion and the Determinate Sentence: Its Distribution, Control, and Effect on Time Served." *Crime and Delinquents*, 24(1978):428–445.

CZAJKOSKI, EUGENE H. "Exposing the Quasi-Judicial Role of the Probation Officer." *Federal Probation*, 37(1973):9–13.

EVANS, WALTER, and GILBERT, FRANK S., JR. "The Sentencing Process: Better Methods Are Available." *Federal Probation*, 39(1975):35–39.

KERPER, HAZEL, and KERPER, JANEEN. *Legal Rights of the Convicted*, St. Paul, Minn.: West Publishing Co., 1974.

LIGOTTE, ALAN J. "Extra-legal Factors in Chicago's Criminal Courts: Testing the Conflict Model of Criminal Justice." *Social Problems* 25(1978):564–580.

ORLAND, LEONARD, and TYLER, HAROLD R., JR. *Justice in Sentencing*, Mineola, N.Y.: The Foundation Press, 1974.

ROBIN, GERALD D. "Judicial Resistance to Sentencing Accountability." *Crime and Delinquency*, 21(1975):201–212.

ROCHFORD, ROBERT E. and ESPEY, LOWELL. "The Sentencing Provisions of the Proposed Federal Code." *Criminal Justice Quarterly*, 6(1978):74–82.

ROSZEL, C. THOMSEN. "Confidentiality of the Presentence Report: A Middle Position." *Federal Probation*, March, 1964, pp. 8–10.

SULLIVAN, DENNIS C., and TIFFT, LARRY L. "Court Intervention in Corrections: Roots of Resistance and Problems of Compliance." *Crime and Delinquency*, 21:213–222.

WILLICK, DANIEL H.; GEHLKER, GRETCHEN; and WATTS, ANITA MCFARLAND. "Social Class As a Factor Affecting Judicial Disposition." *Criminology*, 13(1975):57–77.

THE CORRECTIONAL ROLE OF THE COMMUNITY

Members of a community contribute to the quality of justice they experience. The following seven cases and reading will allow you to relate to correctional situations from a variety of community perspectives. The parent of a juvenile offender, the school teacher who has a disruptive student, the minister who has a parishioner that is an ex-offender, and the community halfway house director all present possible solutions to correctional problems in their communities.

A reading on diversion of offenders and community resources as an alternative to traditional criminal justice process is included at the end of this section.

The Minister and the Ex-Offender

As one of your community's leading ministers, you have always spoken out for progressive correctional reform. Your congregation has usually backed you, and on the few occasions when they did not, they still remained tolerant of your views. Now, however, things are different. Sally, a former member of your church, was once active in working with the church youth. She has since been convicted of embezzlement from the local bank where she worked and sentenced to a year in prison.

As her minister, you kept in contact with her from the beginning of her imprisonment. No one ever really believed she would have to serve time; since the money was returned, no one expected that her boss would even bring charges against her. Everyone has financial burdens at one time or another, and Sally had experienced a succession of problems over a long period of time. The clincher was her husband's permanent disability as a result of an accident. The bills began to pile up faster than she could get them paid. They had mortgaged their house and sold one of their two cars. Finally, in desperation, Sally "borrowed" several thousand dollars from the bank where she had worked as a teller for years. When her crime was discovered, her world crumbled around her.

She has now returned to the community after serving a prison term for embezzlement. When you talked to her the day after she returned, you realized that she was a broken woman. Her daughter had dropped out of school to care for the father, and his disability check was their primary source of income. You counseled her and encouraged her to try and regain her place in the community. You also helped her find work and had even suggested that she return to your church where she had previously been very active. She was reluctant to rejoin the church, fearing rejection by the congregation. You tried to reassure her that everyone was behind her and wanted her to return to the church. In fact, a substantial number of the members had told you as much. When you learned that there would soon be an opening in the Sunday School for a youth director, you asked Sally to consider taking the position. After several days of thinking about it, she agreed.

You have now brought her name before the Sunday School Committee and ·they have, to a person, refused to allow her to be the youth leader. Their bitterness has taken you totally by surprise; their words remain all too clear in your mind: "How would it look to the rest of the community to have an ex-convict directing our youth?" Should you fight for what you believe is right and risk dissension or even possibly splitting the church, or should you tell her that her fears are more valid than you had thought; that her former fellow church members have not been able to forgive and forget?

INSTRUCTIONS:

Decide on a course of action.

A. Carefully define the problem.
B. List all the options or choices you can think of.
C. Rank these options in order of priority.
D. Select the option that you think is the best and briefly discuss the probable consequences.

Parent of a Delinquent

Everyone in your town knows you as "Coach Rowe," a successful and respected football coach. Your son, Jim, is a bright, articulate and handsome high school student. His grades do not reflect the intelligence with which he was gifted, but rather the shrewd manipulative qualities that he has developed. Jim made his grades with ease, but only becaue he was able to con his teachers and to stay out of trouble with you. Perhaps the problem arose because Jim did not have the athletic prowess to excel, or because he found at too early an age that he could get what he wanted without having to work for it; by age thirteen he had developed a long record of problems with the police. The fact is that had he not been your son, Jim would have been adjudicated delinquent a long time ago and probably sent off to the juvenile training school. At the first offense, the police merely brought the boy home, telling you that he had been picked up on complaint from the druggist for stealing comic books, but that they were sure you and the druggist could take care of everything. Jim denied any guilt and you chose to believe him. He did not make restitution on the offense or on the many others that followed. Time after time the police would politely refer the case to you and you would assure them that you would "take care of the matter." In fact, the many disclaimers and excuses Jim's agile mind manufactured continued to sharpen his manipulative skills as he grew older.

Jim had as much success with others as with you. His bright personality and straightforward explanations usually succeeded in removing him, at least partially, from blame; as a result, his offenses seemed to become more serious and more frequent.

One night when football practice was cut short because of extremely cold weather, you were surprised to see Jim loitering in the locker room. Since he never visited football practice, it was unusual to see him there. When you asked what the purpose of his visit was, Jim answered that he was waiting to meet someone. The person he was to meet was not someone you knew, but the parcel protruding under Jim's overcoat prompted another question. "What are you carrying in the package?" you asked. "Just some library books I checked out a while ago," he replied nonchalantly. This was a good enough answer except that you knew the library had closed at noon that day due to a malfunction in the heating system. "Let me see what you are reading, son," you said firmly. Jim realized that there was no point in continuing. Producing an eight-inch brown paper wrapped cube, Jim told you he really did not know what was in the package, but that he thought it was probably a library book; he was just waiting to deliver it for a friend. "In fact," Jim continued, "if it was mine, I would look in it. I am kind of curious." He was all smiles and confident; you wavered, then quickly replied, "Okay, let's see what's in it." The package was heavy to be so small, weighing at least three or four pounds. "Dad, we shouldn't do this; we ought to respect other people's property," Jim protested. Nevertheless, you seized the package and sat down on a locker room bench to unwrap it. The tightly packaged brown waxpaper cubes inside alerted you to what you already suspected, but did not want to believe. From a teacher drug education session, you knew you probably had a small fortune in brown Mexican heroin or something very similar. You also knew that the implication of your son in such a large-scale transaction would mean a trip to the training school or worse, the waiver of jurisdiction by the juvenile court, and trial as an adult as provided in serious felonies. Jim, of course, feigned horror at discovery of the contents and could not identify either the person from whom he received the package or the person to whom he was to deliver it, except to say the recipient's name was Sam and that he would ask for a package. Jim added that he was only doing it for a ten dollar bill and that he was totally ignorant of knowledge of the contents of the package. In fact, he was highly indignant that anyone would take advantage of him in this manner.

Needless to say, you were stunned, but pieces of a puzzle began to fall in place. Jim's girlfriend had dropped out of high school and had somehow acquired a new car. In addition, Jim had received an expensive wristwatch as a present from her. At least Jim had said that is where it came from. Perhaps she is the one who is responsible for Jim's criminal activity or perhaps she is just a "front" for Jim who has graduated into the "big time." You feel sick inside. You know this is something you cannot "take care of." Is this your son standing in front of you, or a stranger? You are beginning to wonder if it is too late to salvage your son and your self-respect as a father. You could turn Jim in and hope for the best, or, on the other hand, you could dispose of the drugs and seek professional help for Jim. You're torn between the two options.

INSTRUCTIONS:

Decide on a course of action.

A. Carefully define the problem.

B. List all the options or choices you can think of.

C. Rank these options in order of priority.

D. Select the option that you think is the best and briefly discuss the probable consequences.

The Correctional Volunteer

Your job with the Department of Corrections is interesting and somewhat frustrating. While the community pays a great deal of lip service to the general idea of rehabilitation, there is a strong undercurrent of retributive feelings, especially noticeable in businesspeople who control the community's finances and therefore have a great deal of influence upon community attitudes.

You knew that being a volunteer coordinator was going to involve motivating people, but you did not expect such passive ambivalence toward community correctional programs on the part of those who comprise the community power structure. Obviously, you will have to get your program going without much help from the city fathers. You ask yourself, "Where do I start on a problem like this?"

Herbert Smith has been a history teacher in the high school for twenty-two years and is well respected by his former students and those in the local business community. Mr. Smith has also taught the adult Sunday school class for fifteen years and has been known to speak out in his low-key way about human rights and other issues involving the dignity of people. You are meeting at Mr. Smith's home to discuss the problems you are encountering as a correctional volunteer coordinator.

Mr. Smith is quite supportive of your ideas, and as you had hoped, he agrees to become a member of your volunteers in parole group. To your surprise, however, he expresses an interest in adult parolees rather than youth, saying that he would like to try his hand with a new group.

Although it is hardly necessary, you do a routine records check with the local police and find that Mr. Smith has not even had a parking ticket in the past twenty years. He looks like an ideal volunteer, and if he is successful, there should be many others.

The first parolee to come to your district who needs volunteer help is Mary Moss. Mary is thirty-eight years old, white, has no family, and has been in and out of correctional programs since she was twelve. She is thoroughly institutionalized and feels that "worse things can happen than going back to prison." She has been involved in numerous and various offenses: larceny, forged checks, shoplifting, receiving stolen property, and too many drunk and disorderly charges to count. Her latest charge was attempted murder; she stabbed another woman during a confrontation in a bar over who had rights to the affection of a certain bartender. Mary's adversary almost died, and Mary drew another prison term.

Mary's former employer, the manager of a small restaurant where Mary has worked as a short order cook on three different occasions, characterizes her as "a good worker, not too smart, smart enough to do what she is told, but not smart enough to stay out of trouble." Mary is not unattractive; although a little on the plump side, it was easy to see she had not been a bad-looking woman when she was younger. She was presentable, but gave the impression she did not quite have it "altogether." Perhaps Mr. and Mrs. Smith could take her case.

After reading her file, Mr. and Mrs. Smith agreed to work with Mary. They sat down with you to work out a residence and employment plan. Mary would be released in ten days; the arrangements had to be completed prior to release to meet the conditions of the parole agreement.

Like all inmates about to be released on parole, Mary had some new prison-made clothes and fifteen dollars in cash from the inmate welfare fund. The state had furnished a bus ticket, as stated in the statute, to "a residence of her choice within the state or to the state line." Mary also had a small, inexpensive vinyl suitcase that she had purchased with earnings from the sale of some of her ceramic dolls in the prison craft shop.

Mr. Smith's attempts to locate a residence for Mary revealed that few rental units were within her means and that all wanted a month's rent in advance, except some residential motels which were operating on the fringe of the law and which would not qualify as an appropriate residence anyway. The problem was compounded by the fact that Mary would normally not receive a paycheck for two weeks which meant that somehow she had to survive until payday. Mr. Smith persuaded the local restaurant manager where Mary was to be employed as a cook to advance her part of her first paycheck in order to help make her situation easier, but even so, the hourly rate which she would be paid was not much above the poverty line. Since Mr. Smith was unable to make arrangements for a satisfactory residence for Mary, he and his wife prepared the back bedroom in their house as temporary quarters for her. After talking to you regarding this arrangement, Mr. Smith decided to charge Mary a token weekly rental fee for the accommodations to promote her self-reliance, and if she was so inclined, to let her work it out by helping his wife with the housework on her days off.

Mary seemed to become like a member of the family, spending most of her time at the Smiths' home when she was not working and seldom going out. She carefully observed the Smiths' house rules, and on her infrequent nights out was always in by eleven o'clock.

When four months had passed, you asked Mr. Smith when he expected Mary would get out on her own. Smith explained that Mary was welcome to stay as long as she wanted, and that he and his wife considered her a part of the family. In the meantime, several other members of Smith's Sunday school class have joined as volunteers in parole, and you have recruited half a dozen other persons as well. The program is slowly gaining momentum, but is still a long way from becoming a full-fledged community effort. You are concerned about the example the Smiths are setting as volunteers. If all your volunteers begin to "adopt" their charges as Mr. and Mrs. Smith have done, not only will there be too few volunteers because of the lack of turnover in volunteer supervision, but further, there will be very little reintegration of the parolee into the community as an independent, contributing member. You feel now that Mary will live with the Smiths until they force her to leave, which at this time is quite unlikely. You want to consider the Smiths' feelings as well as Mary's needs. Still, you feel strongly that a parolee ought to be independent after two months. It is a delicate situation and you are not sure what would be best for everyone concerned.

INSTRUCTIONS:

Decide on a course of action.

A. Carefully define the problem.
B. List all the options or choices you can think of.
C. Rank these options in order of priority.
D. Select the option that you think is the best and briefly discuss the probable consequences.

The Teacher and the Delinquent

Schools have certainly changed since you sat in the classroom. It used to be short hair, no jeans, no slacks, and no fun! One of the reasons students looked forward to college was that they could do and dress as they pleased. But now high schools are becoming very similar to college in many respects. Such traditional concepts as study hall and home room are beginning to disappear. Many high schools allow students much more flexibility in choosing the courses they take, which is a pleasant change from the school system you recall attending. You remember well how much you hated the conformity. Not only are students now allowed more freedom in choosing courses, but teachers are also allowed more freedom in experimenting with different teaching methods. Being a twenty-six-year-old first-year teacher with a newly earned Master of Education degree, you have a number of ideas on how to improve the quality and interest of classroom instruction. Your husband, a city engineer, cautioned you not to expect too much too soon; nevertheless, you remained optimistic about the possibilities regarding innovative educational techniques.

You found out quickly that some of the changes in contemporary high schools might not have been for the better. When you attended high school, the teacher was considered "boss" and his word was usually law. For those few students who did not accept it, there was a wooden paddle available to help convince them. Now, however, paddling a student is rare, even though student discipline continues to grow worse. In fact, your school principal, who believes in paddling as a last resort, has been brought to court twice over such incidents. Because the judge in your community believes in the propriety of selective paddling, the principal won both cases. However, student behavior has continued to become more aggressive in your high school, as demonstrated by several recent physical assaults on teachers.

You are currently faced with a significant discipline problem in one of your own classes. A thirteen-year-old male student has consistently refused to cooperate with you regarding course assignments and behavior in the classroom. At times he is belligerent, and at other times he simply ignores you. Needless to say, such behavior encourages other members of the class to be disruptive also.

This particular student has been in trouble with the police since he was ten years old for truancy, occasional shoplifting, and minor vandalism. You have heard that the juvenile court judge has indicated that one more incident will send him to training school for a long stint.

The principal has agreed to paddle the student or to have him expelled from school; expulsion would probably result in his being sent to training school.

You are uncertain as to what course of action to take. You would hate to see the student sent to training school, but you doubt that paddling would do any good. On the other hand, you can accomplish very little in class as long as he continues to misbehave.

INSTRUCTIONS:

Decide on a course of action.

A. Carefully define the problem.
B. List all the options or choices you can think of.
C. Rank these options in order of priority.
D. Select the option that you think is the best and briefly discuss the probable consequences.

A Family of Offenders

Jake is thirteen years old, a little small for his age, yet wise in the ways of the world and tough as a marine drill sergeant. Jake's usual racket is "protection." For a portion of the other sixth-graders' lunch money, Jake will guarantee that they will not be harassed by the playground bullies, of whom Jake is the most likely hazard.

Since being assigned as a juvenile aftercare worker in the county youth court, you have already seen Jake on several occasions and have heard many stories about his family, which your counterpart in the adult court calls "a breeding ground for felons." If Jake's early conduct is any indication, he will deserve the description of "felon" as soon as the youth court statutes allow.

Jake was not thought to be a proper candidate for a foster home or a group home, so he was committed to the state juvenile training schools on three occasions. His commitment did not seem to have any effect on his subsequent conduct, except that his grades improved after each period.

You decided to visit Jake's home to talk to his mother. It is well known that six of Jake's eight brothers and sisters have served jail sentences, and two brothers are presently in the state penitentiary. Sam, the oldest, is twenty-two years old and is serving eight years for armed robbery. Richard, age nineteen, is serving twenty years for kidnapping and attempted rape of a high school girl who was walking home from school. Jake's two sisters, ages seventeen and eighteen, have long records of shoplifting. The older one was involved in a killing at a local lounge and may be indicted at the next grand jury term.

The specific reason you decided to visit Jake's mother is that he has been associated with a group of four older boys, two of whom are believed to be his brothers, and who are thought to be involved in a series of local "lovers' lane" robberies. The robbers always leave the scene on foot. On one occasion, a fourth member of the band, acting as a lookout, ran up to the three who were committing the robbery to warn them of an approaching car. Although identification was incomplete, a composite sketch created a strong implication that Jake was the lookout. The rest of the gang had worn stocking masks.

Jake's family lives in a three-room flat in the ghetto. Mattresses crisscross the floor of the common bedroom, and there is a new color television, "a gift from a friend," his mother said, in the living room and kitchen combination. The third room appeared to be the mother's private bedroom.

The house was dirty, and the furniture in the main room gave the feeling of a waiting room rather than a family-centered area. You gathered that mama was probably in business for herself, and that it was up to the three children who remained at home to take care of themselves. You doubted that your talk with Jake's mother would produce anything except evasiveness and hostility.

Jake's mother, obviously just out of bed for your 1:00 P.M. appointment, was belligerent and denied any possibility that Jake could be in any trouble, or even heading for trouble. She finally admitted that Jake had been in trouble "once or twice," and then became abusive, blaming the police for her son's trouble. She asked you unceremoniously to "get out and don't come back."

About a month later, Jake and his brothers were arrested by a police undercover team posing as a lovers' lane couple. The juvenile court waived jurisdiction, and Jake was sent to adult court. Although the court-appointed defense attorney attempted to have Jake tried separately he and his brothers were tried together, and all were sentenced to a term in the state prison for adult males. Because of his youth, Jake's sentence was suspended. You are asked by the adult probation supervisor to help with Jake's supervision (both adult and juvenile probation functions are integrated under the same authority in your state). Although Jake is legally bound to serve an adults' sentence and is responsible to the adult court, you may hold the key to his eventual rehabilitation, or there may be no such key. You want to salvage Jake from a career of crime but the "odds" do not look good. Is there anything you can possibly do, or should you just write Jake off?

INSTRUCTIONS:

Decide on a course of action.

- A. Carefully define the problem.
- B. List all the options or choices you can think of.
- C. Rank these options in order of priority.
- D. Select the option that you think is the best and briefly discuss the probable consequences.

Halfway In—Halfway Out

You were originally hired as a unit counselor at the state penitentiary. When the current work release statute was enacted, you immediately asked to be transferred to the new unit. The idea of a counseling situation that centered around "free world" problems rather than the dead end artificiality of the prison environment presented a welcome change. Besides, the new position would also help you to develop a more well-rounded career in corrections.

Bob Sinks was selected to head the new work release program. He had come up in the correctional hierarchy through prison security, and he was considered an expert in his field. Bob was also well liked in the community. His special talent for community relations was just what seemed to be needed for a new community release program.

The new facility consisted of renovated county correctional housing located on the edge of the city and could accommodate eighteen to twenty residents comfortably. Bob's regulations, when they were finally published, were to the point: inmates were to be in by 7:00 P.M. each night and were to be released for work no earlier than 7:00 A.M.; the state bus, clearly marked "state penitentiary" with security wire over the windows, was to be used for transportation. All wages paid to the work releases were to be sent by the employer to the State Penitentiary Prisoner Work Release Fund; a certain portion would be withheld for room and board, and the remaining earnings would be returned to the inmate. Although the procedure was simple and apparently useful, it caused a two-week delay in the releasee's receipt of his pay.

Although the first group of work releasees were volunteers, the eligibility criteria were such that only the prisoners most likely to succeed were selected for the program. The assignment process included both psychiatric and psychological tests, plus restrictions against convicted drug dealers, sex offenders, and certain other dangerous types of recidivists. In short, there was a built-in success factor to facilitate community acceptance.

As one of the new halfway house counselors, you see that problems are beginning to develop. Work releasees on shift work continuously have difficulty making the hours set for the institutional curfew. The prisoners have trouble shaking their "convict" identity on the job. Being carried to work in the prison bus is embarrassing to most of the releasees and almost impossible for those persons on shift work. Furthermore, the food is bad and getting worse. The rations are the same as those at the penitentiary, but prepared by "good security risks" who cannot cook; the best cooks are too valuable at the prison to send to a small community operation.

It is important to you that this halfway house be successful, since you have always been a believer in community corrections. The morale of the work releasees is rapidly deteriorating, and there are even some rumors of escape attempts which, if they occurred, would be sure to end the program by destroying community support.

You want to remedy some of the problems, but first you must talk to Bob. This will not be an easy task, since some of the problems arise from the regulations Bob established. You think you know what needs to be done, but how do you convince Bob?

INSTRUCTIONS:

Decide on a course of action.

A. Carefully define the problem.
B. List all the options or choices you can think of.
C. Rank these options in order of priority.
D. Select the option that you think is the best and briefly discuss the probable consequences.

Probation Officer: Law Enforcement or Treatment?

The court has sentenced Leroy Smith, age nineteen, for the second time in less than a year. The first conviction was for unlawful possession of marijuana. When Leroy's mother testified that he was needed to help support the family, the judge suspended the confinement and ordered Leroy to six months' probation. He was ordered to report to you, state probation officer for the Sixth Judicial District, as you deemed necessary for his restoration to the community as a productive member. The judge agreed that if the probation was satisfactory and Leroy did not get into any more trouble, he would consider expunging the record, since Leroy was only eighteen years old with no previous convictions.

The probation period went well and the court duly expunged the record, but in less than six months Leroy was back in criminal court for the second time. On this occasion he was charged with breaking and entering, a lower degree of burglary in your state. The judge was somewhat exasperated, but considering the fact that this was officially a first offense, he again suspended Leroy's sentence and ordered him to serve four years of supervised probation and make restitution in the amount of value of the items stolen. You felt that the term was somewhat severe, but you know that male offenders in Leroy's age range usually need a great deal of supervision and typically have a higher probability for repetitive criminal behavior than some other groups, and also that burglary is a highly repetitive crime under any circumstance.

Your review of the presentence investigation indicated that Leroy's father disappeared when Leroy was fifteen years old. Soon after the disappearance, Leroy dropped out of high school for a job to help support his mother and his four brothers and sisters. You also noted that Leroy had no juvenile record and still lives at home in a very small but clean apartment in a government subsidized housing project. His is the only income the family has aside from the food stamp supplement.

Your first interview was with Leroy and his job foreman, since the need of income was a primary consideration in suspending the sentence and imposing probation. Leroy's foreman assured you that Leroy was a good worker, and despite the fact of Leroy's long absence from the job while in jail awaiting trial, the foreman readily agreed to take Leroy back. Leroy also seemed to have a good relationship with his boss and coworkers.

You then visited Leroy's mother in an effort to capitalize on the strong mother-son relationship as an aid in reinforcing a responsible behavioral pattern, especially concerning Leroy's after-hours activities. Leroy's mother seemed to blame her son's criminal activity on a bad crowd in the neighborhood with whom Leroy had recently begun to associate.

As a result of weekly consultations with Leroy and his mother, Leroy appeared to be meeting the conditions of his probation with only minimal difficulty. Unfortunately, apparently because of the love of excitement with his new associates and the easy money to be gained, Leroy was on the court docket again twelve months later, this time for conspiracy and burglary of a railway freight car.

The railway police, noting a huge rise in rail cargo theft, had employed extra security officers to stake out the rail yard under increased but discreet observation in an effort to break up some of the gangs that were looting the boxcars. Leroy was caught on a Saturday night with three friends after breaking into five boxcars. Although nothing was missing from the boxcars, Leroy eventually admitted his intent to steal and implicated his companions in a similar manner.

Because of Leroy's cooperation during the investigation, the district attorney decided not to prosecute the case against Leroy, and you decided not to seek a revocation hearing. In addition to other considerations, Leroy seems seriously interested in a girl friend and you believe he just might make a new start if given another opportunity.

About a week after your decision to give Leroy another chance, you are summoned to the chambers of the judge who sentenced Leroy. He demands to know why you did not advise him of Leroy's problems and why he did not get a probation violation report on the matter. He also aks why you were not "on top" of the situation, since he considers monitoring a probationer's behavior and knowing his whereabouts to be a part of your job. You have not always advised the judge of probation infractions that did not involve a conviction, and you are surprised that he is so adamant regarding this one. After all, the state probation officer's manual clearly establishes your duty to seek the rehabilitation of the offender in the best interest of the community and the offender as you see it, which is exactly what you had tried to do. Besides, you find it difficult trying to be both police officer and counselor. However, the judge is quite upset and you are not really as confident concerning Leroy's rehabilitation potential as you would like to be. You have to answer the judge and your own conscience. How do you really feel? What will you say?

INSTRUCTIONS:

Decide on a course of action.

- A. Carefully define the problem.
- B. List all the options or choices you can think of.
- C. Rank these options in order of priority.
- D. Select the option that you think is the best and briefly discuss the probable consequences.

The Diversion of Offenders

Robert M. Carter, D. Crim.

Director, Center for the Administration of Justice
University of Southern California, Los Angeles

Diversion is increasingly being suggested as a viable alternative to traditional processing of offenders through the criminal justice system. This article is in two parts. The first segment attributes the current emphasis on diversion to three factors: (1) increasing recognition of deficiencies in the nonsystem of justice, (2) rediscovery of the ancient truth that the community itself significantly impacts upon behavior, and (3) growing demands of the citizenry to be active participants in the affairs of government. The second section identifies major unresolved problem areas in the diversion process, such as the absence of guidelines for diversion, fiscal complexities, political and social issues, inadequate and uneven community resources, lack of assessment or evaluation of diversion programs, and the need for redefining traditional roles.

I. ORIGINS OF DIVERSION

Although there is considerable discussion and writing by academicians, administrators, and researchers about the system of criminal and/or juvenile justice, the United States does not have a single system of justice. Each level of government, indeed each jurisdiction, has its own unique system. These many "systems"—all established to enforce the standards of conduct believed necessary for the protection of individuals and the preservation of the community—are a collectivity of some forty thousand law enforcement agencies and a multiplicity of courts, prosecution and defense agencies, probation and parole departments, correctional institutions and related community-based organizations. It is clear that our approach to criminal and juvenile justice sacrifices much in the way of efficiency and effectiveness in order to preserve local autonomy and to protect the individual.

Federal Probation, Dec. 1972, pp. 31-36. Reprinted by permission.

The many systems of justice in existence in the United States in the early 1970s are not the same as those which emerged following the American Revolution. Indeed this two-hundred-year evolution has not been uniform or consistent; some of the innovations and changes in our systems have been generated by judicial decisions and legislative decrees; others have evolved more by chance than by design. Trial by jury and the principle of bail, for example, are relatively old and date back to our European heritage in general and the English Common Law in particular. Probation and parole began in the nineteenth century and the juvenile court is a twentieth century innovation.

Coupled with the numerous criminal and juvenile justice arrangements in the United States and their uneven development is the separation of functions within the systems. There are similar components in all systems ranging from apprehension through prosecution and adjudication to correction. Although in fact interwoven and interdependent one with the other, these components typically function independently and autonomously. This separateness of functions, which on one hand prevents the possibility of a "police state," on the other leads to some extraordinary complex problems. Not the lest of these is that the systems of justice are not integrated, coordinated, and effective entities, but rather are fragmented nonsystems with agencies tied together by the processing of an increasing number of adult and juvenile offenders. These nonsystems are marked by an unequal quality of justice, inadequate fiscal, manpower and training resources, shortages in equipment and facilities, lack of relevant research and evaluation to provide some measure of effectiveness and, until recently, a general indifference and apathy on the part of the public which the systems were designed to serve.

Society Itself Contributes to Criminal Behavior

Society deals with crime in a manner which reflects its beliefs about the nature and cause of crime. Many centuries ago, for example, when crime was believed to be the product of the possession of the mind and body by an evil spirit, the primitive response was simple: drive the devil out of the body by whatever means were available for such purposes. The American tradition as relates to the etiology of crime has focused, until recently, upon the individual as a free agent—able to choose between good and evil and aware of the differences between right and wrong. Our "treatment" of crime accordingly reflected the simplistic notion that criminality was housed solely within the psyche and soma of the offender. Regardless of whether the prevalent philosophy was revenge, retaliation, retribution or rehabilitation, the individual was seen as being of primary importance.

We have long assumed that the criminal or delinquent either willfully disregards legitimate authority by his illegal acts or suffers from some personal defect or shortcoming. There is much to learn, however, about the mysteries by which a society generates abnormal responses within its own circles. But this has become increasingly apparent: Society itself contributes significantly to such behavior. Indeed, it is the self-same social structure expressing its force and influence in an ambivalent manner which helps create on one hand the conforming individual—the person respectful of the social and legal codes—and on the other the deviant and lawbreaker who are disrespectful of the law. We have only recently become aware that crime and delinquency are symptoms of failures and disorganization of the community as well as of individual offenders. In particular, these failures may be seen as depriving offenders of contact with those social institutions which are basically responsible for assuring the development of law-abiding conduct.

Note, for example, that it has become increasingly common to discuss the "decline in respect for law and order." In every quarter, and with increasing intensity, we hear that the citizenry, for reasons as yet unclear, is not only failing to honor specific laws, but also displays a mounting disregard for the "rule of law" itself as an essential aspect of the democratic way of life. But even as this concern is echoed, it is not clear that we are all agreed as to what is meant by "decline in respect for law and order" or precisely to whom or to what we are referring. It may be that a large amount of what we observe and label as "disrespect for law" in a wide range and diversity of communities is in fact a normal reaction of normal persons to an abnormal condition or situation.

As knowledge expands to recognize the role of society in the creation of deviance, justice systems themselves will be modified. The implementation of knowledge, of course, always lags behind the development of knowledge.

Mass Disaffection by Large Segment of Population

Concurrent with the recognition that (1) the justice system is but a nonsystem and (2) the community itself has an enormous impact upon the crime problem, there has been—particularly within the past decade—the emergence of mass disaffection of a large segment of our population. This disaffection with the American system is often described in terms which suggest that citizens are not involved in decision-making and are acted upon by the government rather than impacting upon government. The disaffection has been manifested in many communities and in various ways.

We have, for example, been witness to mass civil disorder unparalleled in recent times. We have seen our young people in revolt against the war in Vietnam, the grape industry, selective service, marihuana laws, prison administration, presidential and congressional candidates, Supreme Court nominees, and Dow Chemical. We have observed rebellion against the establishment ranging from burning ghettos and campuses everywhere to looters in the North, freedom riders in the South, and maniacal bombers from East to West. Young and old, black and white, rich and poor have withstood tear gas and mace, billy clubs and bullets, insults and assaults, jail and prison in order to lie down in front of troop trains, sit-in at university administration buildings, love-in in public parks, wade-in at nonintegrated beaches and lie-in within legislative buildings. The establishment has been challenged on such issues as the legal-oriented entities of the draft, the rights of blacks to use the same restrooms and drinking fountains as whites, the death penalty, and free speech. Young people have challenged socially oriented norms with "mod" dress and hair styles, language, rock music, and psychedelic forms, colors, and patterns. We have seen the emergence of the hippy and yippy, the youthful drug culture, black, yellow, red, and brown power advocates, and organizations such as the

Panthers, Women's Lib, the Third World Liberation Front, and the Peace and Freedom Party.

But this disaffection or unrest is not restricted to youth alone. Increasingly, adults are rebelling against the system. One need look no further than the recent slowdowns, work stoppages, and strikes of such tradition-oriented groups as police and fire officials, military personnel, social workers, school teachers, and indeed even prison inmates. Adult participation in protest has generally been more moderate than that of youth; some have been through membership in political organizations of a left wing orientation; others have joined conservative right wing organizations such as the Birch Society or Minutemen. Millions of Americans protested against the political establishment by voting for a third or fourth party or not voting at all in the last presidential election.

Movement Toward Diversion

These three phenomena—recognition that the community impacts significantly upon behavior, the uncertainty as to the effectiveness or quality of justice in the nonsystem of justice, and the growing desire of the citizenry for active, relevant and meaningful participation in every area of governmental affairs and community life—are moving the responses to the challenge of crime in a new direction. This direction is typically referred to as "diversion" and relates specifically to movement away from the justice system. It is most likely a prelude to "absorption" . . . a process in which communities engage in a wide variety of deviant behavior without referral to or only minimum interaction with the traditional establishment agencies.

Diversion is justice-system oriented and focuses upon the development of specific alternatives for the justice system processing of offenders. The diversion model and its application has been generated from a belief that the control of crime and delinquency would be improved by handling criminals and delinquents outside the traditional system. Diversion is also predicated upon the reported effects of the "labeling" process and the impact of the "self-fulfilling prophecy." Whether diversion, at long range, is more effective than the established justice system and whether the "labeling" and "self-fulfilling" phenomena are operationally significant is unclear. These uncertainties do not dictate against diversion models, but rather should serve to restrain unbounded enthusiasm based upon belief and emotion rather than fact.

Absorption may be defined generally as the attempts of parents, peers, police, schools, and neighborhoods to address social problems—including those of crime and delinquency—by minimizing referral to or entry into one or more of the official governmental agencies designated to handle those manifesting deviant behavior. If there has already been a referral, absorption involves the removal of the transgressor from the official processes by offering solutions, techniques or methods of dealing with him outside of the usual agency channels. Absorption is not restricted to the criminal offender or delinquent. It is, for example, equally applicable to deviants within the educational process. Absorption is adaptive behavior within the community in which alternative strategies are developed for coping with social problems. These involve the extensive use of community and personal resources.

II. DIVERSION: SOME PRACTICAL/OPERATIONAL ISSUES

There are issues about diversion—involving both philosophy and practice—which demand in-depth examination. Failure to address these completely interwoven issues is likely to result in diversion efforts which are every bit as fragmented and disjointed as those justice system practices which, in some measure, led to the diversion movement. Rather clearly, there is a need to explore operational aspects of diversion, examine the community, its role and resources and determine the latent and manifest impact of diversion on the justice system. These requirements are in fact mandates for assessment and evaluation. There is an explicit need to: (1) Determine the guidelines and standards which define those eligible or ineligible for diversion, those agencies which are appropriate to receive those who are diverted, and programmatic activities of the agencies which receive diverted cases; (2) identify or develop, and mobilize, resources in a community, determine techniques for increasing community "tolerance" levels, enhance the delivery system for these resources, and make more equitable the availability of resources to diverse types of communities; (3) determine the impact of diversion practices on the justice systems overall as well as their component parts and examine the need for possible administrative, organizational and legal changes; (4) prepare a complete methodology for evaluating the effectiveness of diversion, keeping in mind that being "progressive" is not synonymous with being "successful."

The need for diversion guidelines is critical. Without some minimum standards for practice and procedure and general consensus or agreement on philosophy, there is a distinct possibility that diversion may become the source of continuing and substantial inequities. Basic questions—such as who is (or is not) to be diverted, by whom, on what basis, and to what programmatic activities—should be answered by some shared understandings. Without such common understandings, the justice system—through increased use of nonsystematic diversion—may become more confused, autonomous, and fragmented.

Some minimum standards are needed, for example, to guide the *selection of individuals* for diversion. Diversion practices may be exclusionary and identify types of offenders who are deemed ineligible, such as those with a history of violence or felony offenders. Or practice may be permissive and allow that all offenders who will benefit from nonjustice system treatment are to be considered eligible, regardless of other considerations. Diversion may be restricted to adjudicated offenders, or it may include nonadjudicated offenders. If the former, diversion is from the system after entry; if the latter, diversion is an alternative to entry into the system. Both raise substantial legal issues.

Determinations as to time frames are required, i.e., the optimum time for diversion, the length of time or duration of diversion, and so on. Guidelines are also needed as to actions to be taken if the person diverted fails to comply with the actual or implied conditions of diversion or if it appears that the diversion plan is inappropriate.

Meaningful standards are necessary, for the *selection of agencies* to receive those who are diverted. Diversion need not necessarily be made to private agencies; it may be appropriate for there to be diversion to those public agencies which normally have been either minimally or not at all concerned with the offender population. And it may be appropriate for diversion to be to individuals rather than agencies. The selection of agencies requires community inventories which in turn may indicate the need for new private and/or public agencies or combinations/consortiums/conglomerates of established agencies which address needs of offenders.

Of equal significance is the complex and politically sensitive problem of sifting through a wide variety of potential diversion agencies including those with "unusual" or nontraditional characteristics such as those with an ex-offender or ex-addict staff. Underlying many of these guidelines are fiscal considerations—including possible requirements for subsidies to agencies which handle those who are diverted. A delicate issue arises from public support of private agencies in terms of performance objectives and standards, constraints and expectations. The subsidy issue is made even more complex as the need arises to determine which public agency at what level of government pays the subsidies to these new partners in the justice system.

There is, of course, a requirement to examine the *programmatic activities* of the agencies which receive diverted offenders. While an inventory of these various programs and some estimate of their effectiveness are essential to rational diversion practice, a basic question emerges as to whether offenders should be diverted if appropriate (or at least similar) programs exist within the justice system. And if such programs already exist in the justice system, the advantages, if any, which accrue by transfer of these programs and clientele to community-based, nonjustice system organizations must be established.

The movement of programs and offenders to nonjustice system organizations will require new roles for justice and nonjustice system personnel. As an example, the probation or parole officer realistically might be required to become a catalyst and seek to activate a community and its caretakers to absorb the offender as a member of that community. This would require a complete knowledge of community resources and diagnosis of clientele needs. There would be an emphasis on reducing the alienation of the offender from his community by impairing the continued maintenance of a criminal identity and encouraging a community identity. The officer would no longer find employment for the offender, but instead direct him into the normal channels of job seeking in the community. Residential, marital, medical, financial or other problems would be addressed by assisting the offender to engage those community resources which deal with these problem areas. This new role, then, might be one of insuring a process of community, not correctional absorption. Again illustrating interrelationships of these issues, note that the "new role" phenomenon itself raises questions about training for and acceptance of the role and methods or techniques of implementation.

Imbalance in Community Resources a Problem

Other issues arise as one examines the role and resources of the community. Not at all insignificant is the complex issue of imbalance among communities to accept cases which are diverted and to provide necessary services and resources. Some communities have distinct economic advantages over others—and it is clear that diversion has an economic, as well as a motivation base. Middle- and upper-class communities and their citizens, socially and economically secure, often have internal financial resources available to mobilize a wide range of agencies of diversion or specialized services ranging from psychiatric care through private schools. The differences in resource levels need scrutiny, for it would be socially disastrous to deny diversion to those who are economically disadvantaged; diversion cannot be restricted to the affluent. Without action to balance resource requirements with the capacity of delivering services, the poor and the disadvantaged will continue to flow into and through the justice agencies.

A parallel community-based problem occurs where there is a low community tolerance for diversion. How is community tolerance to be increased? A simple demonstration of need may be insufficient. Numerous examples of low or nontolerance may be cited ranging from open through latent resistance and hostility directed against self-help groups and agency halfway houses. And besides the very difficult "how," there is the related question of "who" is responsible for dealing with community fears and anxieties. Is every justice agency seeking to divert offenders responsible for its own resource development or is some overall plan among cooperating justice agencies more rational? And again, as one question leads to another, if a plan is necessary, who designs and implements it, and how are activities financed and monitored?

Diversion Will Result in Significant Changes

Although changes in justice systems are inevitable consequences of an increased use of diversion, there is a distinct probability that the changes will be both unplanned and unsystematic. These changes may range from administrative and organizational restructuring and modification in procedure and policy on one hand through major changes in the populations which are serviced by the justice systems on the other.

As justice agencies become partners with communities, there may be requirements in all agencies for organizational change to include new bureaus or divisions of "community service." This would require new personnel or reassignment of personnel, development and acceptance of new roles such as those of diagnostician and/or catalyst, innovative training, perhaps additional funding and different kinds of facilities, and new understandings within the agencies and communities themselves. Permanent linkages with community organizations may re required. Traditional pyramid, hierarchical organizational models may have to be flattened. New information systems will be required, and continuing involvement or monitoring of diverted cases may be desirable.

The large-scale diversion of offenders—either from or after entry into the justice system—may have other consequences for the justice agencies. If, for example, substantial numbers of offenders are diverted by local law enforcement to community-based agencies, there will be, in all likelihood, reduced inputs to prosecution, adjudication and correctional agencies. Lessened inputs will alleviate some of the backlog in the judicial system and reduce caseload pressure in probation and parole and size of institutional population. While these occurrences are desirable, at some point in time the bureaucratic instinct for survival may be threatened. Reactions protective of the establishment may set in. Of greater significance, however, is that increased diversion may leave the justice system with a unique clientele of hardened, recalcitrant, difficult offenders who seem unlikely to "make it" in the community. These offenders may have complex problems requiring long-range treatment and they may represent a major threat to and be rejected by their communities. In addition to creating major management problems, these offenders will require new and different programs, facilities and staff for treatment. In short, extensive diversion may not only "threaten" the justice establishment, it may change the justice system population and alter the system itself.

Planning and Evaluation Necessary

There are yet other important aspects of diversion which require attention—planning and evaluation. A lack of mid-range and strategic planning and systematic evaluation has long been a major defect in justice operations from law enforcement through corrections. The movement toward diversion of offenders mandates that planning and evaluation not be "tacked on" to operational processes, but rather be built-in, continually updated, constantly reviewed. The questions about planning and evaluation are familiar—criteria must be established, funds must be made available, personnel, software and hardware must be obtained, methodologies developed, responsibilities delineated. Without such planning and evaluation, it appears certain that diversion practices will produce more confusion and chaos than clarity and consistency.

Conclusion

This article has explored the origins of diversion and identified some of the major operational and philosophical problems associated with the movement. Diversion is seen as an outgrowth of a fragmented justice system which has been neither just nor efficient, the increasing demands of our citizenry to be participants in the affairs of government including the justice system, and recognition that the community is an appropriate base for many justice operations. But even as there is increasing momentum toward diversion, there is a pressing need for guidelines, standards and shared understandings, examination of the role and resources of the community, study of the long-range impact of diversion on the justice system and society, and planning and evaluation.

Diversion is both a challenge and an opportunity. As a potentially major mechanism of the justice system, diversion requires considered attention. Although changes in our justice systems are indicated, rapid movement to untested and ill-defined alternatives is inappropriate.

Selected Bibliography

CARNEY, LOUIS P. *Corrections and the Community*. Englewood Cliffs, N.J.: Prentice-Hall, 1977.

CARTER, R.M. "The Diversion of Offenders," *Federal Probation,* 36(1972):31–36.

DRESSLER, DAVID. Probation and Parole: Companion Services." *Probation and Parole,* New York: Columbia University Press, 1969.

FLYNN, LEONARD E., and DUSSICH, JOHN, P.J. "Divergent Roles of Volunteers in the Criminal Justice System." *L.A.E. Journal,* 39(1976):2–7.

HARLOW, ELEANOR; WEBER, J. ROBERT; and WILKINS, LESLIE T. *Community Based Correctional Programs: Models and Practices*. Rockville, Md.: National Institute of Mental Health, 1971.

HART, WILLIAM. "Oklahoma's Down Home Parole Board." *Corrections Magazine,* 4(1978):54–59.

HOREJSI, CHARLES. *"Training for the Direct-Service Volunteer in Probations."* *Federal Probation,* 37(1973):38–41.

KILLINGER, GEORGE G.; KERPER, HAZEL B.; and CROMWELL, PAUL F. JR. *Probation and Parole in the Criminal Justice System*. St. Paul, Minn.: West Publishing Co., 1976.

MUNN, DALE. *Intervening With Convicted Serious Juvenile Offenders*. U.S. Department of Justice, July 1976.

RUTHERFORD, ROBERT BRUSE, JR. "Establishing Behavioral Contracts With Delinquent Adolescents." *Federal Probation,* 39(1975);28–32.

SACKS, MASON J. "Making Work Release Work: Convincing the Employer." *Crime and Delinquency,* 21(1975):255–265.

SCHOEN, KENNETH F. "The Community Corrections Act." *Crime and Delinquency* 24(1978):458–464.

SCOTT, RONALD J. "Contract Programming in Probation: Philosophical and Experimental Bases for Building a Model." *Justice System Journal* 4(1978):49–70.

SMITH, DAVID LEWIS, "Public Opinion and Penal Policy." *Criminology,* 14(1976):113–124.

SOLWAY, KENNETH S., HAYS, J. RAY, and ZIEBEN, MARIL U., "Personality Characteristics of Juvenile Probation Officers." *Journal of Community Psychology,* 4(1976):152–156.

TOMAINO, LOUIS. "The Five Faces of Probation." *Federal Probation,* 39(1975):42–45.

WARREN, DONALD I., and WARREN, RACHELLE B. "A Community Leader's Handbook: Different Strokes for Different Neighborhoods." *Psychology Today,* June, 1975, pp. 76–80.

WATERS, EUGENE J. "Community Oriented Correctional Programs: The Social Ecology of a Restitution Shelter." *Journal of Humanics,* 5(1977):35–45.

WEINTRAUB, JUDITH F. "The Delivery of Services to Families of Prisoners." *Federal Probation,* 40(1976):28–31.

WENK, ERNST A. "Delinquency Prevention Models in Schools." *Juvenile and Family Court Journal,* 29(1978):17–27.

WELLFORD, CHARLES F., and WIATROWSKI, MICHAEL. "On the Measurement of Delinquency." *Journal of Criminal Law and Criminology,* 66(1975):175–188.

THE INMATE

The next seven cases and the reading will provide you with insight into the world of inmates in prison. All types of persons are present in an inmate population; there are good and bad persons—some who feel a great deal of remorse for their offenses and others who seem to feel no remorse for their crimes. Bullies, drug abusers, embezzlers, as well as former school teachers, lawyers, and doctors comprise the typical prison population. To gain maximum understanding of the inmate in prison, you should attempt to relate to each case as if you were the inmate who is described. The solutions to the problems raised in these cases will become more significant as you put yourself in the inmate's place.

A reading is included at the end of this section which discusses problems in dealing with inmates as though they were abnormal.

Bust or Parole?

Your name is Harry. You are forty-five years old and have served twelve years on a twenty-year sentence for armed robbery. This is the second time around for you. The last time you were in the "joint" was for burglary; you did three years on that sentence and made parole. You stayed straight for almost two years before you got into trouble again. Several of your drinking buddies finally convinced you to go along as the driver on an easy bank score. Unfortunately, it did not turn out to be so easy. The bank's security officers opened fire on your two friends as they left the bank, killing one of them and wounding the other. You quickly surrendered without a struggle. You knew armed robbery was not for you, and you have always regretted your involvement in that particular event. In fact, you have been regretting for twelve years.

The twelve years you have served on your present sentence have not been easy ones. The inmates in the prison you are in are of a new breed, generally younger and more militant. Violence on the inside has increased; there are more rapes, suicides, and assaults than ever before. Although the years have been hard, you have tried to make the most of them. You have earned your high school diploma and have even taken several additional college level courses in accounting. Your brother, who owns a small business, has offered to employ you if you make parole. With your good behavior, your personal efforts toward rehabilitation, and your brother's offer, your chances of making parole are excellent. You realize that you have got to stay straight this time or resign yourself to spending most of your remaining years in prison. You really want to make it this time, but there is some trouble brewing in your cellhouse that could blow your chances for parole sky high and even pose a threat to your own life.

A great deal of illegal drug activity is going on in your cellblock. Although drug traffic in most prisons is rather common, in your institution, the correctional officers are heavily involved in the illicit drug sales and distribution. In fact, rumor has it that the Chief of Security is behind most of it. The word is also out that regular and undercover state narcotics agents are presently conducting an investigation. The problem is compounded for you since your cellblock is the site of the majority of drug activity. You have considered going to the prison Superintendent, Dr. Smith, who you are certain is not involved in the drug traffic. You know him to be an experienced and progressive corrections administrator who has increased the rehabilitation opportunities for you and the other inmates. You are really beginning to get uptight because the prison grapevine says that a bust is imminent. Since your cellmate and other inmates in your cellblock are heavily involved in drugs, you could be implicated by association. You can sit tight or go to Dr. Smith and tell him what is going on. You wonder whether or not you can really trust the Superintendent. If you do tell him what is going on, will he believe you? Will he return you to the cellblock to be at the mercy of those inmates and correctional officers you reported? A bust might well ruin your chances for parole. A trip to Dr. Smith might help your chances for parole or, on the other hand, endanger your personal safety.

INSTRUCTIONS:

Decide on a course of action.

- A. Carefully define the problem.
- B. List all the options or choices you can think of.
- C. Rank these options in order of priority.
- D. Select the option that you think is the best and briefly discuss the probable consequences.

Six Months to Go

Six months ago the biggest concern in your life was finishing college. Now your biggest concern is your own personal safety. Never in a million years did you dream that you would be spending the twentieth year of your life in a state prison. As a sociology major in college you studied about crime, criminals, and prisons, but it was nothing compared to the real thing. The constant noise of steel and concrete; the smell of bodies, cigarettes, and old buildings; the inability to go where you want to go, eat what you want to eat — all this is foreign and confusing to you.

Sure, you smoked some grass and sometimes used pills to stay up and study for exams when you were in college; a lot of other students did the same. You had never expected to get "busted" with just three joints. But you did. Since it was your first offense, your lawyer said probation was a sure thing. Unfortunately for you, however, you got a judge who was fed up with drug abuse. He decided that it was time to crack down, and he used you for an example. As a result, he sentenced you to three years in the state prison. When he pronounced sentence, the sky fell for you and your family.

Your experiences in prison have left you confused and frustrated. During those first few months of incarceration, you felt hopeless and alone. Your family, although upset and embarrassed, has stuck by you. It was the efforts of a young prison counselor and the support of your family that have kept you going. Only six months remain on your sentence before you come up for parole. You have "kept your nose clean" with the prison staff and other inmates.

Last night a terrible incident occurred: Your eighteen-year-old cellmate, Sam, was brutally raped and beaten by four older inmates, who informed you that the same fate would be yours if you reported them. You remember only too well the whistles and the threats directed toward you during the first several days you were in the cellblock. You realize that your size and former athletic conditioning allowed you to establish a relative amount of independence in the prison; your cellmate, being smaller and weaker, had no such natural defense qualities. You also realize that if you report what they did to your friend, the four inmates are likely to make good their threat. Still, you cannot rid yourself of the rage and sickness you feel because of your friend's humiliation and helplessness. You know that he might be attacked again. Yet, you are also confronted with your own needs of survival and well-being.

The only employee you trust in the prison is a young counselor. Not having been at the prison very long, he has only limited influence with the prison administration. Nevertheless, he is enthusiastic and well intentioned. You cannot forget what happened to your cellmate, yet with only six months before parole, you are also thinking of your own welfare.

INSTRUCTIONS:

Decide on a course of action.

  A. Carefully define the problem.
  B. List all the options or choices you can think of.
  C. Rank these options in order of priority.
  D. Select the option that you think is best and briefly discuss the probable consequences.

An Expression of Grief

You are known as Willy throughout the prison and are serving ten to fifteen years on a manslaughter conviction. Before your present conviction, you were sentenced to probation on an assault and battery charge. Now a model inmate, you stick pretty much to yourself and give no one any trouble. Since being in prison you have become interested in religion and spend a great deal of your time reading and studying the Bible.

You recently began receiving weekly letters from your younger sister concerning your father, who was hospitalized again for a terminal liver ailment. Rereading the letters brought back many memories of your childhood. Your father worked long and hard in the coal mines of Kentucky to support his wife and seven children. Although you know you have been pretty much of a failure with your life, you still have a tremendous amount of respect for your father. You decided to request a special pass from the warden to visit your sick and dying father.

The warden considered your request, but felt that your maximum security classification and his own difficulties in having to run a prison that was understaffed necessitated his rejecting it. Needless to say, you were quite upset. You felt frustrated and helpless.

Several days later the sky fell in. You received a call from your sister telling you that your father had died and that the funeral would be in two days. You again approached the warden, to get permission to attend your father's funeral. The warden sympathized with your plight, but again declined your request, for the same reasons given previously. You flew into a frustrated rage and the guards had to subdue you while the prison physician gave you a sedative. The assistant warden in charge of treatment then had a guard escort you to the chapel for personal counseling with the institutional chaplain, Reverend Jones.

You are now waiting for the chaplain. Visibly upset, you remain silent as you sit there by yourself. You know from other inmates that security is weak in this area of the prison. Should you sneak out the back entrance of the chapel and hide in the milk truck that is parked there each morning? Every inmate in the institution knows about this escape route and you now have the opportunity to take advantage of it. What should you do? Sure, they would pick you up in a couple of days, but not before you got home for your father's funeral. Of course, you wouldn't make trustee in six months as the warden has promised. Your positive prison record wouldn't be so positive anymore. But what is more important, your father's funeral or your prison record? You sit there hurt and confused, trying to decide what your next move will be.

INSTRUCTIONS:

Decide on a course of action.

A. Carefully define the problem.
B. List all the options or choices you can think of.
C. Rank these options in order of priority.
D. Select the option that you think is best and briefly discuss the probable consequences.

Something for Nothing

Your name is Billy Denver. Your mother, a registered nurse, divorced your father years ago. Although she had several relationships with other men in the years following the divorce, none ever worked out on a permanent basis. She also had several bouts with alcohol and amphetamine abuse. As if that was not enough, you have not seen your father since the divorce.

You have always had an easy smile. Everyone has always remarked how easygoing you are, how well you roll with the punches. Sure, you have gotten in trouble several times. Once you and two friends were caught joy riding in a car that was not yours, and twice you were apprehended for possession of a substantial quantity of amphetamines. The judge described your third possession charge as the last straw as he sentenced you to nine months in the city jail. You smiled politely as you received your sentence, thinking that the city jail could not be any worse than the boring high school you have been attending.

When you arrived for processing at the jail you were surprised and confused at the whistles and catcalls the other inmates gave you as you walked with the guard through the recreation yard to your cellblock.

Eighteen years old, with long straight hair and a fair complexion, you just smiled back and gave the peace symbol in hopes of letting the other prisoners know that you wanted to get along with them.

The next morning the control station guard sounded the bell and opened the gates as the inmates poured out of their cells heading for the chow hall. Since you were not hungry you decided to stay in your cell and read a western you had borrowed from one of your cellmates.

You look up from your book to find a big burly inmate standing in your doorway. "Hi kid," he says with a cold stare.

"Hello. My name is Billy Denver," you respond, eager to make your first friend.

"I know," the visitor replies. "My name is Tom. Most guys in here call me 'Big Tom'." He goes on to explain to you that things are different in jails and prisons, in ways that people on the outside cannot understand. He continues to stress that in order to have a "safe stay," it is best to have good friends that will stand up for you.

Although you do not completely understand what Big Tom is trying to say, you are relieved at having made a friend so quickly. Tom notices the book in your hand and inquires if you like to read. You indicate that you do and that you hope to read your way through your sentence if you can get enough books. Big Tom assures you that you will not have any problem getting books, since he is personal friends with the jail's librarian. As he describes the kinds of books he likes to read, Tom reaches into his shirt pocket and pulls out a pack of cigarettes. Lighting one, he asks you if you smoke. "Only menthol," you reply. Tom assures you that he can supply you with plenty of menthol cigarettes, since the guy who works in the inmate canteen owes him a number of favors.

As Tom turns to leave, he says, "It gets very lonely in here, Billy, and we have to take care of each other. Just remember, Big Tom takes care of his own. You just be my friend." Needless to say, you are a little overwhelmed by his concern and generosity concerning some of the things he said to you. Should you respond to his friendship? He does seem to know the ropes. What will happen if you decide to remain somewhat aloof and do your time by yourself?

INSTRUCTIONS:

Decide on a course of action.

A. Carefully define the problem.
B. List all the options or choices you can think of.
C. Rank these options in order of priority.
D. Select the option that you think is best and briefly discuss the probable consequences.

Showdown at Seven o'Clock

You have been in the state prison for six years. Most of the black inmates in your prison recognize you as their leader, a status which has been yours since one night when the former leader tried to set you up in the showers. It was an unfortunate incident, especially for him. Having been tipped off, you and several of your friends got the best of him and his henchmen. You were injured in the fracas, and he was killed. The results of the whole mess were that you received two additional years for voluntary manslaughter and that you emerged as the primary black leader for the inmates in your prison. The additional time did not mean that much to you, since you were already pulling two concurrent life sentences for a previous shootout on the streets where two bank guards were killed. For many reasons you did not really want the leadership role, but there were some advantages to it. Besides the respect of the other inmates, life in general was a little easier. Being on top brought special favors from the other inmates and special consideration from the correctional staff as well.

In the two years you have been the leader, you have had to deal with a number of problems and issues, including militant young blacks, the Black Muslims, and rival groups. The white inmate group called "The Brotherhood" has created the most problems for you. There have been several confrontations with them, complete with bloodshed and death. In spite of these conflicts and a rigid and disinterested warden, for the most part, the lid has been kept on the prison. In a strange way you are proud of your efforts toward keeping some measure of peace among the various inmate factions. You are especially proud of how you and the white inmate leader helped the administration avert a major racial confrontation when the prison cellblocks were forced to desegregate by federal court order. You even received a special letter of commendation from the State

Corrections Commissioner. But all that was yesterday. Now another confrontation is building up.

Young militants in your group and the white group are planning an all-out war over the use of the prison band instruments. Your group's "soul" band and the white group's "country and western" band have always had something of a running feud, but now the situation has gotten out of hand and is about to explode. You and the white inmates' leader, Tom, would like to avoid the bloodshed of an all-out riot. However, both of you are having trouble controlling the younger inmates in your respective groups, and the prison administration is not providing much help. In fact, word has come down from the warden that it is up to you and Tom to control your people. The showdown is to take place at seven o'clock in the dining hall. You want to avoid bloodshed, but you also have to maintain the confidence of the black inmates you represent. Tonight in the dining hall all hell may break loose! You cannot back down, and compromise is becoming more difficult as seven o'clock draws nearer. The minutes are ticking away.

INSTRUCTIONS:

Decide on a course of action.

A. Carefully define the problem.
B. List all the options or choices that you can think of.
C. Rank these options in order of priority.
D. Select the option that you think is best and briefly discuss the probable consequences.

What's for Supper?

Your name is Harriet, but most of the other girls at the state women's prison call you Sis, an affectionate nickname you have earned because you have been a "big sister" for most of the girls in the prison, especially the younger ones. You come up for parole in two months and you have been told that your chances are good. You have done three years on a five-year sentence for voluntary manslaughter. You have relived the event many times in your nightmares. One of the many drunken squabbles between you and your husband ended with you holding a gun in your hand and him lying dead on the floor. Although the nightmares still come from time to time, you can live with what happened now. It is behind you. Besides, you have a nine-year-old daughter who is living with your mother and waiting patiently for your return. Helping the other girls at the prison has been therapeutic for you. You are proud of their confidence in you and your established reputation of being firm but offering an understanding ear.

The food at your institution has never been good, but now it is becoming unbearable. The meals consist mostly of starches; meat is served infrequently, and is always of inferior quality. The poor selection of food is bad enough, but the preparation is even worse. Since you are a respected leader of the other inmates, it fell to you to go to the prison superintendent and complain. She assured you that the food quality would significantly improve, but it had not. You wonder why not. Maybe it was not her fault. Maybe it was a problem of the chief cook's. Maybe the state did not allow enough money for an adequate diet.

Whatever the reasons were, tensions continued to mount. For many of the girls, mealtime was the high point of their day. The repeated disappointment of receiving stale bread, gristle instead of meat, and not enough coffee created a potentially explosive situation. Each mealtime in the dining hall was becoming more tense. There had already been several minor confrontations between the inmates and the guards.

Now a group of the girls have asked you to endorse a dining hall protest over the poor food. Because of the high level of emotions, you realize that the protest could easily escalate into a full-blown disturbance. You are sitting on a powder keg that could explode during any meal. You know there is reason to protest, but you also realize that if a serious disturbance occurs, you and the others might lose more than you could ever hope to gain. On the other hand, the superintendent and her administration have failed to make any significant improvements regarding the food quality. If you do not support the protest, you might lose the respect of the girls. If you do support it, you might all lose. Should you approach the superintendent again? Should you just sit tight and see what happens? Should you go ahead and endorse the protest hoping that it remains peaceful? There is no easy way to go, and time is running out.

INSTRUCTIONS:

Decide on a course of action.

A. Carefully define the problem.
B. List all the options or choices that you can think of.
C. Rank these options in order of priority.
D. Select the option that you think is best and briefly discuss the probable consequences.

Home Sweet Home

Next Wednesday you will be walking out those front gates as a free man. This last time around cost you ten years. It was your third hitch. You have spent thirty of the last forty years of your life behind bars. Sixty-two years of life's ups and downs has softened your disposition. You have no excuses left; you feel that the time you got was coming to you. In fact, the last hitch was one you purposely set up.

You had been released on a cold gray morning in February. There was no one on the outside waiting for you; your friends were all in prison. You had been divorced for over fifteen years and your former wife had remarried. Your parents were dead, and your two sisters had given up on you long ago. Besides, there were too many decisions to make in the free world. You were not use to all of that freedom; it was frightening. No one cared about you like they did inside the joint.

You got a job as a busboy in a restaurant, but the hustle and bustle was too much, and besides, no one wanted to make friends with an old ex-con. Finally you had all you could take, so you stole all the money from the cash register one night during a lull in the business. You did not spend any of it, but instead went home, had a beer, and waited. In less than two hours, the police arrived at your apartment. Once the restaurant manager realized you and the money were missing, it was not long before you were arrested. You refused an attorney and told the judge that you would keep committing crimes until he sent you back. He reluctantly sentenced you to ten years. You passed up parole each time it came around.

So here you are again. You have been measured for your new suit of street clothes and your fifty-dollar check for transitional expenses has been processed. The labor department representative has arranged for you to have a stock-clerk job in a small grocery store in a nearby town. Your social worker has also arranged for you to stay in a small apartment near where you will work. You remember your last prerelease counseling session with her and how she offered all the words of encouragement a young, energetic, and well-meaning counselor could muster. You just smiled and nodded your approval. What good would it have done to burst her idealistic bubble? She could never understand how frightening the outside world had come to be for you. All of her friends lived in the free world; none of yours did.

You would like to make it on the outside if you could, but the odds are against you. And besides, it's just too lonely out there. You know you ought to feel happy about leaving prison, but the truth is, you are miserable about it. You would like to be able to make it on the outside, but deep down inside, you feel you are doomed before you start.

INSTRUCTIONS:

Decide on a course of action.

- A. Carefully define the problem.
- B. List all the options or choices you can think of.
- C. Rank these options in order of priority.
- D. Select the option that you think is best and briefly discuss the probable consequences.

A Basic Error: Dealing With Inmates As Though They Were Abnormal

Elmer H. Johnson, Ph.D.

Center for the Study of Crime,
Delinquency and Corrections
Southern Illinois University, Carbondale

At a time offering remarkable prospects for revitalization of the system of criminal justice, it is useful to examine contemporary correctional practices for major flaws. This article focuses attention on the prison because it has been the primary tool of the brand of penology which is being questioned. We refer specifically to those prisons emphasizing control of inmates through psychological coercion. However, we do not assume the contemporary probation and parole programs necessarily avoid the flaws present in the custodial prison.

In diagnosing inmates and in applying programs described as "treatment," the prison tends to underestimate the operation of sociological variables in the etiology and persistence of criminal behavior. These variables include the many elements of life in the community groups such as the family, recreational groups, and peer groups. In fact, it is assumed that constructive change in offender behavior can be accomplished by cutting him off from the influences of the community. Furthermore, the custodial prison tends to overlook the influences of its own organization on stimulating inmate resistance to the "treatment" programs. Behind these oversights is a simplistic faith that punishment will deter and halt criminal behavior. In lieu of confronting the complexity of the social and psychological forces underlying criminal behavior, the custodial prison relies on this faith to circumvent laborious and patience-taxing effort by attempting to bulldoze behavior change through psychological coercion and suppressive measures.

"CRIMINALIZATION" AND BEHAVIOR SYSTEMS

Criminological scholars have placed increasing stress on two key ideas. First, in speaking of the "criminalization of deviance," they refer to the effect on an individual of the official and public action of defining him as a "criminal."[1] Here the term

Federal Probation, 35 (March 1971), pp. 39-44. Reprinted by permission.

111

"criminal" is used to mean "enemy of society" who is clearly distinct from the "respectable" and "decent" people who behave as law abiding citizens. Conviction in court constitutes an official ceremony announcing that a person has been found to be such a criminal. "Deviance" suggests that there are many degrees of nonconformity ranging from slight variation from expected behavior to outright warfare on the society the law is supposed to safeguard. "Criminalization" refers to the process of lumping all these varieties of deviants into the "enemy of society" category. As in the case of war, the adversary is described in the most negative terms as though he were nonhuman. The differences among the citizens of the enemy nation and their attractive qualities as a population are forgotten in this indiscriminate indictment through wartime propaganda. Similarly, the differences among deviants and their attractive qualities are overlooked when all of them are defined as "criminals." There is an implication of abnormality in the sense of marked and strange irregularity and inferior adjustment to conditions of life.

When the offender does not merit such an extremely negative evaluation, he becomes a victim of this criminalization process which drives a sharp psychological wedge between the "good" people and the "evil" people. He has personal qualities and has engaged in behavior which were not part of the particular situation which brought him before the court. Limiting attention to his behavior in this particular situation has exaggerated the validity of the diagnosis of his total personality on the basis of only a small portion of the facts pertinent to evaluation of him as a total person. He usually does not see himself as an enemy of society. In lumping him with "criminals" with whom he does not identify, the indiscriminate labeling of this kind of offender tends to block his affiliation with law abiding citizens. He is encouraged to think of himself as a full-fledged criminal and as somehow "abnormal" in that he deviates from the norms of "respectable" people.

This article goes beyond the usual application of "criminalization of deviance" to consider also its implications for correctional work within the prison. As we have already noted, all prisoners are subject to being arbitrarily labeled as "abnormal" simply because they have been convicted as criminals. Now we direct attention to the prison as a social world in itself. "Deviants" become those inmates who fail to conform to the expectations of officials. "Criminalization" becomes the process whereby any transgression of prison rules subjects the inmate to the risk of being regarded by officials as a rebel at war with officialdom. The transgression may be incidental to his total behavior within the prison, but exaggerated attention on the transgression erodes the distinctions between him and the genuine rebels. He is tarred with the same brush as the manipulator, the resistant prisoner, the "rat," and other deviant types among prisoners. With the drawing of a sharp line between "good" and "evil" prisoners, he is lumped indiscriminately with those prisoners regarded as exhibiting marked and strangely irregular behavior and inferior adjustment to conditions of prison life. This version of criminalization pushes the rule violator into the status of "abnormal" prisoner regardless of the significance of his transgression and its consistence with his overall behavior in prison. He is encouraged to affiliate himself with the covert or active enemies of officialdom.

Second, the criminal behavior system has been utilized as a typological tool to capture the idea that offenders differ in the significance of their offenses within a sociocultural environment. We shall use the key premises of this typology as a framework for discussing the pertinence of "criminalization of deviance" to the prison. Instead of studying criminals as though they constitute a single species, the criminal behavior system approach distinguishes between several classes of offenders on the basis of certain fundamental premises.[2]

• Offenders are not regarded as generally abnormal in the biological or psychological sense.

• The sociocultural organization of society favors the incidence of certain types of crime.

• As a response to certain segments of the sociocultural organization, criminal behavior leads to similarities in form and scope.

• The offense has varying significance among criminals in terms of their life organization.

"NORMAL" VERSUS "ABNORMAL"

Under the criminal behavior system, offenders are not regarded as universally abnormal in the sense of either peculiar qualities of their physiology or perverse attitudes. Instead, criminality is attributed to learning of behavior in the course of relationships with other persons in the same general fashion as noncriminal behavior is learned. However, some persons become criminal because their particular personality traits are brought in conjunction with standards of particular groups which press them to organize their life around behavior which is defined as criminal by the larger society.

The question of the "abnormality" of the law violator is obscured by the conflict of rules among the various groups which make up society. Is he "abnormal" when he conforms to the expectations of a particular subculture which is considered to be out of step with the standards of the elite which dominates the power structure of the particular community? Is the "perfect father" and "loyal employee" necessarily a pathological being because he is convicted of an offense which came from situational factors in only one segment of his total life activities? Such questions justify more careful study of the assumptions that the convicted person is "abnormal" simply because he has been convicted.

First, his offense sometimes is regarded as evidence that he is totally committed to criminal values and, therefore, is an "enemy of society." This interpretation draws sharply defined boundaries between the "honest citizen" and the "criminal." Conviction for a crime, especially when imprisonment ensues, results in arbitrary labeling of the transgressor as a "criminal," i.e., an "enemy of society."

Second, his imprisonment usually is regarded as evidence that he requires treatment for psychological and/or sociological "abnormality." His offense is taken to indicate that he is "maladjusted," "pathological," or "deficient" in his total life style, reactions to social situations, and his conceptions of his proper behavior in the events occurring in the family, neighborhood, and occupation. "Rehabilitation" then becomes a matter of total revision of his personality and social behavior. This perspective has weaknesses. The offense may not be descriptive of his total personality and his performance in all segments of his life experience. In fact, the offense may be out of gear with his usual mode of behavior. It may provide little, if any, evidence that he is incapable of adjusting satisfactorily with the conditions and circumstances encountered by a person occupying his place in society.

Third, the definition of one group (or one set of values) as "abnormal" implies that at least one group (or set of values) is "normal." The system of criminal justice has been assigned the mission of protecting "society" against crime. This protective function includes safeguarding citizens against physical danger and loss of property. However, protection also involves support for those social norms seen as of key importance in maintaining orderliness in the life of the community. The legal code reflects a selection of particular norms to benefit from this protection. The selective process is dominated by the particular groups which dominate the power structure. A fundamental but hidden assumption is that the selected norms are shared by members of a single society characerized by a single moral perspective. Usually this situation is summarized by the statement that the laws reflect middle class values which are thereby imposed on other social classes. Then, risking oversimplification for the sake of brevity, we say that the expression of middle-class norms in the criminal laws implies their superiority to those of groups which are not middle class in attitudes and behavior.

The official labeling of a convicted law violator as a "convict" brings into play the implication that his behavior is different than that of a so-called normal person, with "normality" usually defined as middle-class behavior. Because of the hidden assumption that the middle-class values expressed in the operation of the criminal justice system are universally supported in society, this identification of the "convict" status with general abnormality ignores the possibility that the offender is adhering in many ways to normal behavior as defined by a particular subgroup. For example, his behavior may be within the range of expectations of ghetto dwellers, fellow excessive drinkers, a segment of some occupational group, a dedicated religious or political minority, and so on.

Recognition of the individual qualities of the offender and the prisoner is a familiar and basic principle at the various stages of the system of criminal justice. The practical implementation of this principle is undermined by the assumption that deviation from the legal norms in and of itself justifies treatment of the offender as a totally abnormal person. In a society composed of a variety of subcultures, this indiscriminate labeling has the unfortunate consequence of providing opportunities for many versions of moral imperialism. Then "rehabilitation" programs are diverted from the specific task of overcoming criminality to the more general task of achieving general adherence by all members of society to a particular moral code. In this case, the offender is only one of several classes of nonconformists, but the system of criminal justice has made him visible and a more controlled target for moral conversion.

Fourth, as a corollary of the third point, the successes of the offender in adjusting to many situations are ignored under the generalized premise of his "abnormality." Criminological literature frequently points out the error in the popular view that residents of slums universally are socially and personally maladjusted. The same general point can be made in reference to arbitrary assumption that the convicted offender is incapable of adjustment to social control. Successful membership in clearly criminal groups, of course, does not qualify an individual for acceptance in prosocial groups. However, even in this extreme example, the convicted offender probably has demonstrated capacity for adjustment to social imperatives to a degree greater than suggested by his nonconformity with certain criminal laws.

Within the prison, certain categories of inmates engage in what appears to be unorthodox behavior. These categories include rebels, "rats," malingerers, "prison-wise" manipulators, and so on. Indiscriminate labeling of these groups as "abnormal" risks the probability that the official responses to their behavior will jeopardize the rehabilitative goal because the improperly labeled prisoner will raise psychological barriers against his own genuine and essential participation in the processes intended to bring constructive change of his own behavior.

In what way is this indiscriminate labeling of deviant inmates as universally "abnormal" invalid? We offer several reasons. In spite of a prevalent view, commitment to criminal values and commitment to the inmate social system are not necessarily identical. Certainly, the two forms of commitment are opposed to the authority of an establishment, at least to some extent, and are usually dedicated to obtaining rewards in manners prohibited by the establishment. Furthermore, the values of the inmate social system intersect criminal values in many respects. Nevertheless, the two sets of values are not necessarily congruent. The problems of social survival and personal gratification within the narrow world of the prison press inmates toward at least tacit compliance with the values of the inmate social system. There are gradations among the degrees of inmate compliance, but, even when the degree is strong, the inmate may comply for sake of contingencies of the immediate circumstances of penal confinement.

Furthermore, inmate transgressions are usually interpreted as evidence of the perpetrator's "abnormality" as a total personality. Because the behavior does not conform to official expectations, it is assumed the deviant is a "maladjusted," "pathological," or "deficient" personality. This assumption implies that the violation of prison rules is solely a product of the inmate's own perversity. However, the act occurs within the social setting of the prison. The search for explanations should include the sociocultural setting and determining conditions found in the prison.

SOCIOCULTURAL ORGANIZATION OF SOCIETY AND THE PRISON COMMUNITY

Now we turn to the second major premise of the behavior system approach. The nature of the sociocultural organization of society affords a setting favorable to the incidence of certain kinds of crime. Since criminals as well as noncriminals are social beings, they are subject to the sociocultural organization of society to a greater degree than the usual conception of them as totally pathological beings would indicate. The characteristics of the sociocultural organization may afford a setting favorable to the incidence of certain kinds of crime.

Similarly, the sociocultural organization of the prison imposes stresses favoring violation of the official norms. The heavy reliance on physical and psychological restrictions by prison administration aggravates the tensions of prison life. The restrictions facilitate the growth of the subterranean social system among inmates. The prison is remarkably deficient in provisions for tension management. As a counter to the power of officialdom, manipulation of circumstances and official procedures for the sake of inmate purposes becomes a way of life. Considering the sociocultural setting of prison, it would be an oversimplification to regard the transgression as "abnormal" simply because its purposes were in opposition to the official social system of the prison.

The inmate social system is as much a sociological reality as is the official system. Prison transgressions are social behavior because the perpetrator is responding to cultural values and the contingencies of special situations. The actor has evaluated his social situation and the qualities of other actors in the situation. His action is based on this evaluation. The interpretations of others affect his evaluation of his current stressful situation and his resort to violation of official rules as a means of adjusting to the specific situations he encounters.

Inmates differ in the status position they occupy in this inmate social structure, causing stress for those prisoners who are either unwilling to accept and/or are denied membership in the inmate social system. In either instance they are denied access to the inmate social structure which provides protection and the subterranean means of gaining privileges and gratifications barred by official rites. They are made more vulnerable to the pressures of confinement as a human experience and to the stresses stemming from other prisons.

If the inmate is affiliated with the inmate social system, he is more likely to engage in aggressive transgressions when he is placed in a position where the inmate social system is not effective in meeting his personal goals. Paradoxically, increase in the pressure exerted on the transgressing prisoner by the officials raises the odds that he will employ extreme measures as an alternative form of adjustment.

RECURRENT BEHAVIOR PATTERNS

As a response to certain segments of the sociocultural organization of the free community, criminal behavior leads to similarities in form and scope. Crimes, such as shoplifting, are perpetrated in repetitive ways. Victims are selected and exploited in particular ways. Certain principles are followed to reduce chances of detection, apprehension, and prosecution. Here the very organization the criminal law is designed to protect becomes a factor in shaping the nature of the violations of that law. This article adapts this point to the inmate deviations from the official rules which serve as the equivalent of law within the custodial prison. The custodial prison paradoxically becomes an agent for creating inmate deviation from the norms the prison attempts to maintain.

The existence of recurrent behavior patterns among prisoners is documented in the literature on their social roles.[3] The very existence of the inmate social system in similar form from prison to prison provides additional evidence. Clemmer has delineated "prisonization" as a social process pressing the inmate toward affiliation with prisoner behavioral codes and he has traced the relationship between this process and certain qualities of the inmate's characteristics and status.[4]

The sociocultural organization of the prison generates the persistence of a contraculture[5] among inmates. The frustrations of confinement create a psychology favorable to hostility to the keepers. The inmate's inferior status reminds him of lawful society's rejection of him as untrustworthy and disreputable. The inmate values protect him from psychological devastation. He is thrust into special intimacy with persons with long records of antisocial and aggressive behavior and who are carriers of prisoner traditions.

A punitive orientation is characteristic of the entire system of criminal justice with the custodial prison serving as its agent. The ultimate goal of punishment is to prevent the prisoner from engaging in future violations of the social norms being safeguarded by the system of criminal justice. In addition to serving theoretically this ultimate goal, the custodial prison has the more immediate purpose of maintaining order among the inmates and gaining conformity to its own set of rules intended to promote the goals of the prison establishment.

The psychological costs to the inmates of a punitive orientation, we noted above, are encouragement of counterculture. In addition, the punitive orientation creates results which stand in stark contrast to the equalitarian ideology of American society. The prison autocracy opposes the democratic principles which are supposed to characterize the life the inmate is urged to embrace in the name of rehabilitation. Beyond this conflict in messages communicated to the prisoner, the inmates experience a discrepancy between what officials say and what is reality when it comes to the relationship between whole-hearted participation in "treatment" programs and regaining of ultimate acceptance as a full citizen in the free community after release.

This discrepancy is a consequence of several factors. The inmate social system defines whole-hearted participation in rehabilitation programs as evidence of "selling out." The main justification for participation is exploitation of opportunity to achieve secondary gain through perversion of the official social system. On the other hand, the official system blocks achievement by inmates of the goals it presents. Rewards are distributed in standardized fashion to the benefit of the inmate clever in manipulation and pretense. Rewards have restricted significance when all inmates experience loss of liberty and status degradation.

CRIME AND LIFE ORGANIZATION

The criminal behavior system approach refers to the varying significance of offenses to the life organization of various transgressors. Although individuals may commit offenses which are legally similar, this behavior actually has different significance for several sociological classes of offenders, even if all would be grouped under a single legal category such as homicide or theft.

Some offenders relegate crime to the periphery of their life organization, while others breaking the same law center their entire life around criminal transactions as primary occupational activities. The housewife may shoplift to gain a few extra luxuries beyond her budget, but she continues to organize her life around the status of respectable housewife. The professional shoplifter engages persistently and systematically in stealing as the prime means of livelihood. In the course of systematic study and practice in shoplifting skills, the professional thief comes to identify himself with certain rationalizations which justify his shoplifting as "moral" and which link him emotionally and socially with other professionals. The linkages are useful, furthermore, in providing a degree of protection against apprehension and a means of team behavior in stealing. However, such affiliations require that the novice gain admittance to the colleague-ship among professional thieves.

The adverse consequences of arbitrary labeling of prisoners as "abnormal" beings are most significant in the pressures they exert on prisoners to move toward centering their lives subsequently around crime. Description of the prison as a "college for crime" usually refers to the teaching of inexperienced inmates in criminal techniques and values by other inmates already committed to criminal careers. Because dedicated criminals compose only a majority of most prisoner populations, we consider this indiscriminate labeling of the inmates as "abnormal" to be more significant than the "schooling" function in making the prison a vehicle for increasing the numbers of dedicated criminals. Indiscriminate labeling encourages the inmate uncommitted to criminal values to be more congenial to the inmate value system and to organize his prison life around these values.

SUMMARY AND IMPLICATIONS

In the long run the reduction in the persistence of criminality is dependent in large measure on successful persuasion of offenders to identify themselves with the social norms the criminal law is intended to safeguard. Using the concept of "criminalization of deviance," we have analyzed ways in which the prison erects barriers by arbitrarily labeling inmates as psychologically distinct from law abiding citizens. The system of criminal justice narrows its conception of the convicted offender by focusing on the offense as characteristic of his general behavior. In implementing punishment as the strategy for halting criminality, the prison expresses the conception of inmates as "abnormal" regardless of his other qualities. Furthermore, in responding to violations of its rules, the prison tends to apply coercion and to regard the transgressor of the prison's social order as perverse.

The rise of community-based corrections has been heralded as a particularly promising answer for the dilemmas raised by the prison. Increased and more effective use of probation and parole is advocated. Local correctional centers would emphasize preservation of the inmate's linkages with the community through training, work release employment, and other uses of local resources. Regardless of the particular strategy employed, emphasis should be placed on those qualities of the offender which promote his identification with the community values with which he is expected to adhere as a law abiding citizen. Our central argument is that special effort is required to minimize the possibility that indiscriminate labeling of the convicted offender as "abnormal" will abort the rehabilitative process. Since this labeling can occur in any of the community-based strategies, the restructuring of the correctional system must involve abandonment of suppressive and coercive measures as the paramount policy. The difficulties of implementing the principle of individualized treatment lie in wait for those responsible for introducing genuine correctional reform in the face of the prevalence of labeling.

NOTES:

1. For example see: Edwin M. Schur, *Crimes Without Victims,* Englewood Cliffs, N.J.: Prentice-Hall, Inc., 1965, pp. 5-6: Howard S. Becker, *Outsiders: Studies in the Sociology of Deviance,* New York: The Free Press of Glencoe, Inc., 1963, p. 9.

2. Among the books dealing with behavior systems are these criminological textbooks: Herbert A. Bloch and Gilbert Geis, *Man, Crime and Society,* New York: Random House, 1962, pp. 577-84; Marshall B. Clinard, *Sociology of Deviant Behavior,* New York: Holt, Rinehart & Winston, 1963, pp. 210-216; Elmer H. Johnson, *Crime, Correction and Society,* Homewood, Ill.: Dorsey Press, 1968, pp. 230-277; Walter C. Reckless, *The Crime Problem,* New York: Appleton-Century-Crofts, 1961, pp. 75-77; and Edwin H. Sutherland and Donald R. Cressey, *Principles of Criminology,* Philadelphia: J.B. Lippincott, 1960, pp. 238-239.

3. For example, see: Gresham M. Sykes, *The Society of Captives,* Princeton, New Jersey: Princeton University Press, 1958; Erving Goffman, "On the Characteristics of Total Institutions: Staff-Inmate Relations," in Donald R. Cressey (ed.), *The Prison,* New York: Holt, Rinehart & Winston, Inc., 1960, pp. 23-48; Gresham M. Sykes and Sheldon L. Messinger, "The Inmate Social System," in Richard A. Cloward, et al. (eds.), *Theoretical Studies in Social Organization of the Prison,* New York: Social Science Research Council, 1960, pp. 5-9.

4. Donald Clemmer, *The Prison Community,* New York: Rinehart & Co., Inc., 1958, pp. 298-300.

5. Melton Yinger, "Contraculture and Subculture," *American Sociological Review,* Vol. 15 (October 1960), pp. 625-35.

Selected Bibliography

ANDERSON, DAVID C. "Co-corrections." *Corrections Magazine,* 4(1978):32−41.

AULT, ALLEN L.; BONNER, JAMES C. JR., and HAMILTON, CHRISTOPHER J. "Legal Aid For Inmates As an Approach to Grievance Resolution." *Resolution of Correctional Problems and Issues,* Spring, 1975.

BECK, JAMES L. "The Effect of Representation at Parole Hearings." *Criminology,* 13(1975):114−117.

BRASWELL, MICHAEL, and CABANA, DONALD A. "Conjugal Visitation and Furlough Programs for Offenders in Mississippi." *New England Journal on Prison Law,* 2(1975):67−73.

BRODSKY, STANLEY L. *Families and Friends of Men in Prison.* Lexington: Lexington Books, 1974.

BRODY, STUART A. "The Political Prisoner Syndrome." *Crime and Delinquency,* 20(1974):97−106.

GLEASON, SANDRA E. "Hustling: The 'Inside' Economy of a Prison." *Federal Probation,* 42(1978):32−40.

GOLDFARB, RONALD L. "American Prisons: Self-Defeating Concrete." *Psychology Today,* January, 1974, p. 20.

GRISWOLD, H. JOLCK; MISENHEIMER, MIKE; POWERS, ART; and TROUMANHAUSER, ED. *An Eye For An Eye.* New York: Holt, Rinehart and Winston, 1970.

GUENTHER, ANTHONY L. "The Forms and Functions of Prison Contraband." *Crime and Delinquency,* 21(1975):243−254.

LENIHAN, KENNETH J. "The Financial Condition of Released Prisoners." *Crime and Delinquency,* 21(1975):266−281.

MARKLEY, CARSON W. "Furlough Programs and Conjugal Visiting in Adult Correctional Institutions." *Federal Probation,* 37(1973):19−26.

MCARTHUR, A. VERNE. *Coming Out Cold: Community Reentry From a State Reformatory*, Lexington, Massachusetts: Lexington Books, 1974.

MCDOWELL, CHARLES P., and THYGUSEN, NORMAN. "The Loser and the Criminal Justice System." *Internal Journal of Criminology and Penology*, 3(1975):155–161.

MEYERS, LOUIS B., and LEVY, GIRARD W. "Description and Prediction of the Intractable Inmate." *Journal of Research in Crime and Delinquency*, 15(1978):214–228.

MAY, EDGAR. "Prison Ombudsmen in America." *Correctons Magazine*, 1(1975):45–60.

PETERSON, DAVID M., and TRUZZI, MARCELLO. *Criminal Life*, Englewood Cliffs, N.J.: Prentice-Hall, 1972.

PRICE, RAY R. "The Forgotten Female Offender." *Crime and Delinquency*, 23(1977):101–108.

SANTAMOUR, MILES B. "The Other Ten Percent." *American Journal of Corrections*, 39(1977):16–36.

SERRILL, MICHAEL S. "Delancey Street." *Corrections Magazine*, 1(1974):13–28.

WILSON, ROB. "Juvenile Inmates: The Long Term Trend is Down." *Corrections Magazine*, 4(1978):3–11.

THE CORRECTIONAL OFFICER

The correctional officer is an important key to the success of any correctional program. Correctional officers are not only responsible for institutional and program security, but they also have tremendous potential as "change agents" of the behavior and attitudes of the inmates they supervise.

In the next seven cases and the reading you will learn of some of the demands placed on the typical correctional officer. Crisis intervention skills, peer group pressures, and riot control are examples of the situations presented to elicit your reaction.

Two readings on the causes of prisoner riots are included at the end of the section.

The First Day

You are a twenty-five-year old correctional officer, and this is your first day on the job. You have recently completed eight weeks of training at the Department of Corrections training academy, where you developed some degree of expertise in such areas as behavior control, communications operations, riot techniques, self-defense, and general security administration. You have also completed two years of college, earning an Associate of Science degree in Criminal Justice, and you plan to continue studying and to earn a bachelor's degree in the same field.

You have been assigned as an officer on the seven A.M. to three P.M. shift in the state prison. This particular prison is a maximum security institution housing about two thousand inmates. The facility was originally built in the early 1930s to house no more than twelve hundred inmates. Besides the obvious problems created by confining too many inmates in too little space, other factors such as poor lighting and ventilation, long narrow corridors, and fortress-like construction have created a rather depressing and negative atmosphere. Because of your education and academy training, you are confident of your ability to perform your assigned duties in a highly professional manner. You feel that you will be able to communicate well with inmates and prison staff alike. In fact, at the academy you were described as one of the "new breed" of correctional officers—better educated, more understanding, and highly competent.

Upon reporting for work this morning, you went directly to roll call. The shift supervisor informed you that since daily work assignments are distributed on the basis of seniority, you will not choose an assignment, but will simply be assigned to duty in the metal trades shop. The other corrections officers then smile and laugh for no apparent reason. Although you had expected a warmer reception at roll call, you tried to shake it off and accept it as a challenge to prove yourself worthy of the other officers' friendship and respect.

Since the supervisor did not bother to inform you as to where the metal trades shop was located, you had to ask another officer for directions. He pointed you in the general direction and left you with the thought that he was glad it was you going back there rather than him. This officer's lack of concern and his implicit warning added to your growing sense of frustration and caused your confidence to begin to deteriorate. You became nervous about being new on the job and even more uncomfortable because no one seemed to care. The academy instructors had told you how to get along with your fellow officers and display a restrained friendliness toward the inmates, but successfully applying their training was proving to be a very difficult task indeed.

Your first eight-hour tour was, to say the very least, filled with bewilderment and disappointment. While on duty in the metal shop, you tried to start a friendly conversation with the other officer on duty; his only response was, "Don't make no unnecessary enemies." Attempts to introduce yourself and converse with the inmates were even more disappointing. If they spoke at all it was to describe you in some unflattering terms.

Your first day of work ends with your having second thoughts about your job, what you are supposed to be doing, and your self-worth in general.

INSTRUCTIONS:

Decide on a course of action.

A. Carefully define the problem.
B. List all the options or choices you can think of.
C. Rank these options in order of priority.
D. Selected the option that you think is best and briefly discuss the probable consequences.

A Legacy of Corruption

You were born and reared in a rural area in the South. Your family was above average for working class families in your town. Your father, a farmer, worked hard and saved his money. As a result he was able to provide you, your brother, two sisters, and your mother with a life of dignity and a sense of belonging — belonging to family, to town, and to country.

There was dignity, but no extras. Work was hard and income uncertain. Great thrift was no mere virtue; it was a necessity. Your parents imbued you with the "American dream" that hard work and education would make your life easier and more productive than theirs had been. By education your parents meant high school and possibly some vocational training.

After high school, you and one of your best friends decided to join the Air Force, enlisting for the full four years. Your tour of duty was rather uneventful, even with the escalation in Vietnam. You were assigned to a base in the North where you were able to learn a trade. Since your Air Force job was in aircraft maintenance, you planned to seek aircraft work when you were finally discharged.

When 1967 arrived and you were discharged, you returned to Midville and your family. This was the time you had been waiting for — you were ready to seek a career and a life of your own. Midville was home to you and you wanted to settle there. There were no aircraft jobs around, but you were offered a job as an automobile mechanic for a local garage. But that was not quite what you wanted; you felt that you would like to do something more meaningful with your life. You wanted a job that would give you both security and a sense of accomplishment. You even considered reenlistment. Then you saw an advertisement:

> Correctional Officers needed at State Prison. Civil service position, fringe benefits, career opportunity. High school required, military obligation must be completed. Beginning salary range $5600 to $6500. Apply at personnel office, main prison.

You knew a fellow who had gone to work in the prison. He seemed to like his job. In fact, many of the local people worked there. It was nearby, had good job security, and seemed to be a worthwhile, respectable occupation. You decided to look into it.

Six weeks later you completed your basic correctional officers' training and with your fellow trainees you took and signed your oath of office as provided for in Section 26 of the state code:

> I do solemnly swear or affirm that I will faithfully and diligently perform all the duties required of me as an officer of the Department of Corrections and will observe and execute the laws, rules, and regulations passed and prescribed for the government thereof so far as the same concerns or pertains to my employment; that I will not ill treat or abuse any convict under my care, nor act contrary to the law, rules and regulations prescribed by legal authority, so help me God.

The years pass by and you find yourself looking at your thirtieth birthday. You are married and have three children of your own and are barely making ends meet financially even though you have eight years of seniority. You have been hoping for a promotion, but none has been forthcoming. You have found that the inmates in your charge sometimes openly ridicule your professional status and pay. Since you are still on the swing shift, you are unable to attend college courses at the Community College twenty-five miles away. The inmates, however, have plenty of free time and are taking college extension courses at state expense right here in the main unit of the prison. Some of them, now college educated, are going on parole to much better paying jobs than you have. Although you like your job and feel that it is worthwhile and a public service, as a dedicated officer, you feel somewhat unappreciated and underpaid for the function you perform. Many of your peers share your occupational dilemma, and some, in fact, are quite bitter about what they consider to be preferential treatment toward the inmates.

Now to increase your sense of frustration, you have learned that your captain and several other of your fellow officers are taking bribes from inmates in exchange for choice assignments. You mentioned to the captain that word has reached you with regard to the purchased assignments. Instead of being embarrassed or evasive, the captain tells you that "These scumbags would sell their mothers for a dime and they deserve whatever happens to them." He then offers to assign you to the unit in charge of housing so that you can "put some steak" on the table for your family. Conflicting needs flood your consciousness. The last officer to complain about this particular captain was summarily dismissed and threatened with prosecution for possession of contraband which he claimed he was not even aware of. The captain's father is also a former warden of this prison, and his brother is the present business manager of the institution.

Needless to say, the situation has created a major crisis in your life. Your decision will be crucial because of its lasting implications for you and your family. You value your personal integrity and you believe in the intrinsic value of your profession, yet you could use more money. Second, there is the pragmatic necessity of your employment and your hope for advancement within the system. What should you do?

INSTRUCTIONS:

Decide on a course of action.

   A. Carefully define the problem.
   B. List all the options or choices you can think of.
   C. Rank these options in order of priority.
   D. Select the option that you think is best and briefly discuss the probable consequences.

Man in the Middle

The memo from the warden is brief and unmistakably clear:

> To all prison personnel:
>   All fighting, assaults, confrontations, loud arguments, and other contentious interactions between inmates are to be reported in writing at the end of each shift. Participants are to be placed in administrative segregation for not less than forty-eight hours; work assignments are to be changed to less desirable ones; and letters describing each incident will be placed in the inmate's file and with the parole examiner's file. There will be no exceptions.
>
> The Warden

The above letter is the policy statement that you and your fellow officers have just received. The policy clarification is in response to increasing violence within the institution that has resulted in the injury of seven inmates and two officers during the month of July alone.

It is a good memo, supportive of staff, and appropriate at this time because violence between inmates has escalated and needs to be curbed. You are happy that the officer's individual discretion has been removed and that inmates who are put on report will not be able to take you to task for disciplinary action. A penalty is required and you have no choice.

Your assignment within the institution is "A" wing, a dormitory unit which consists of special housing for prison aides. Prison aides work irregular shifts, night shifts, or in the hospital and, consequently, are often on call. They are presumed to be more trustworthy; hence, the special housing and more flexible hours. Several of the inmates in this dormitory are administrative and one of them, Browning, probably typed the Warden's memo on fighting.

You are working the graveyard shift, 11:00 P.M. to 7:00 A.M. On Tuesday, shortly after midnight, you hear a disturbance and run immediately to the dormitory. From the corridor you turn on the overhead dorm lights. Inside, two inmates are crouched, ready for combat, on opposite sides of a single bed. Both are armed with sharp objects and are slashing at each other as they move from left to right around the bed. The rest of the inmates, though reluctant to get involved, have now seen you. They are divided, with one group enjoying the diversion and wanting the action to continue, and the other group wanting to settle the fight. The combatants are also aware of your presence, but continue to circle and glare. You quickly run to the end of the narrow corridor and call for help. Returning to the dorm, you find that the inmates have returned to their respective beds and all weapons have disappeared.

The confrontation is over and you are the only observer. One of the men involved is an aggressive homosexual and former weight lifter who is head baker for the staff dining room. The other person involved is the head clerk for the Chief of Prison Security. Both offenders are eligible for parole in a few months.

At this point the lieutenant arrives to find no disturbance; instead, he finds the quiet of a hot summer night and you in a state of frustration. "Inmates Smith and Taylor were fighting, sir," you state. "They had weapons. I'll write up the report." The Lieutenant ponders a moment. "Well, come on over to the office and let's talk about it." As you approach the office, the lieutenant says, "Look, Bill, you know nothing important happened. Let's not stick our necks out. It's hot. Arguments are bound to happen; it's over now. If you report this, these guys will be denied parole and it'll mean grief for us all." You agree, but point out the recent directive on violence from the warden. "Well, do what you want," the lieutenant says, "but I advise against it."

You are now having difficulty in deciding what to do. If you do not report the incident, you will satisfy your lieutenant, who is your immediate supervisor, but might risk the wrath of the warden. Furthermore, if the warden learns of your failure to report the fight, the lieutenant probably will neither back you nor admit that he advised you to violate the directive. Also, the inmates who know of the directive will know that you deliberately violated a major policy. If you report the incident, you will anger the lieutenant and probably not gain any favor with the warden, since he usually hears only of violations of his directives rather than complaints.

Paradoxically, the Warden will more than likely hear of the incident, since all of the inmates in the dormitory work with and for the administrative staff. Grapevine communication in the prison is quite active and very little goes unnoticed. You also worry about the example you set for the inmates when you do not observe written rules. You wonder if they will lose respect for you if you do not write up the incident.

There is something else to consider. If you do write the report, it is sure to anger some of the inmates, particularly Browning, the clerk who types in the warden's office. Browning is the boyfriend of one of the participants, the weight lifter, and is sure to be angered if his boyfriend loses his parole and his job in the prison bakery. The civilian food service manager will also be angry, since he will have to train a new bakery chef.

You believe that rules are necessary if there is to be order in the prison. You believe that directives, if legal, should be obeyed consistently and without reservation. If a directive is inappropriate, you believe that it should be challenged openly in a reasonable way. But you also feel thta you must try to get along with the people you work with.

You are the man in the middle. No matter what you do, you are going to upset somebody. You must make a decision, even if it is a decision to make no decision.

INSTRUCTIONS:

Decide on a course of action.

A. Carefully define the problem.
B. List all the options or choices you can think of.
C. Rank these options in order of priority.
D. Select the option that you think is the best and briefly discuss the probable consequences.

More Education: For Better or Worse?

Even though you finished only one quarter of college work, you liked the idea of a degree; it was just that college did not seem as important as Elaine. You did not want to stay at the truck stop forever. You were not sure what you wanted to do for a lifetime career, but you were pretty sure that your future was not one of changing tires on eighteen wheelers. What was merely an indefinite idea or hope that you would someday have a good job became something of a necessity when Elaine delivered the ubiquitous and inevitable announcement. It seemed like a surprise, but there was no need for shock; nothing could be more natural than that Elaine would become pregnant.

The news that soon there would be three prompted you to do some real thinking about your future. You had heard a friend of yours talking about getting on at the prison as a guard. After you were there for a year, they would even help you go to college. They had good employment benefits: insurance, paid vacations, and job security.

You began thinking ahead rapidly. You could begin as a guard, get a degree from the community college, and maybe even be a warden someday. The next morning you went to the prison personnel office to submit an application. The prison official in charge of personnel was polite, told you about all the state benefits, and eventually sent you to be interviewed by the Chief of Security.

The chief leaned back in his swivel chair. "What makes you think you can handle convicts?" he solemnly asked. You quickly responded, "We talked about prisons in a social problems class I had in college. Prison work seems to offer a challenge and a future. I would like to study corrections and someday even be a warden." The chief, still leaning back in his chair, stared at the butt of his well-chewed cigar for several moments and finally said, "Well, the warden hasn't quit yet, but out here we see a college education and one year of experience as being about the same thing. Ain't no social workers on my crew. If you want to do a job, keep your nose clean, and keep the convicts on the job and in their place, I'll give you a chance. But,'' and here he became most emphatic, ''I don't want no social workers or other hot shot college graduates on my staff!''

You were discouraged by the chief's attitude, but felt that time would eventually prove the value of education, so you took the job. The job itself was quite routine. Four weeks on day shift, four weeks on evenings, and four weeks on midnights. Time passed faster on the day shift; men going to and from work, men being released and admitted—there was always something to do. Midnights were slow, and there was little to do but make rounds. You used the time to study. You liked your work and wanted to know more about corrections. You had enrolled in the community college and had begun studying correctional administration. In the beginning, your sergeant and immediate supervisor had agreed that he would try to arrange your schedule so that you could attend classes at the community college. However, when you actually started your coursework, it seemed to enrage the sergeant. ''I can't reschedule the whole prison so you can go to college! What the hell do you need to go to college for? We don't need more college kids. We need some more people with some common sense! If college is so important, why don't you quit and become a fulltime Rah-Rah boy? I may have to find someone who is more interested in his job than in getting a piece of paper!'' You felt like quitting, but you liked the work and, even more important, you needed the job.

You have three more years of college before you can complete your bachelor degree requirements. When you have accomplished that goal, you can qualify for a variety of ''treatment'' or ''administrative'' positions. The problem is that you are not sure whether or not you will last that long on the job. You always thought education was a good thing, but under the present circumstances you are beginning to wonder. You also have your family's welfare to think of.

INSTRUCTIONS:

Decide on a course of action.

A. Carefully define the problem.
B. List all the options or choices you can think of.
C. Rank these options in order of priority.
D. Select the option that you think is best and briefly discuss the probable consequences.

An End, or a Beginning?

You have been a correctional officer at the state prison for three years. You have had your ups and downs, but the job has always been interesting. For the last year you have been in charge of Cellhouse B, which is home for one hundred adult male inmates.

Fifteen minutes ago you made your hourly check around the cellhouse, and since everything appeared to be quiet, you returned to your desk which was located near the main entrance gate. You had just begun making headway with some overdue paper work when several inmates at the far end of the cellblock began yelling for you to come quickly.

Upon arriving at the scene of the disturbance, you found a twenty-six-year-old inmate who had been incarcerated about six months semiconscious with a sheet tied around his neck and looped around an overhead steam pipe. With the help of a nearby inmate you untied the sheet from the young man's neck and laid him on his bed. After calling on the intercom to the medical section for assistance, you returned to the young inmate, who had by then regained full consciousness.

While waiting for him to be transported to the prison hospital, you attempt to carry on a conversation in an effort to help him relax. The results of your efforts are surprising. Although depressed, the young inmate begins to openly discuss his problems with you. It is apparent that he trusts you, but you ae becoming increasingly unsure as to how you should handle the situation. You are not a professional counselor, and perhaps you are venturing too far out of your area of expertise.

Should this young inmate be a problem just for the prison counselor or psychologist, or should you allow yourself to become involved with him, with his problems and his feelings? One part of your instincts tells you to keep your distance, while another part tells you to help him if you can. What should you do?

INSTRUCTIONS:

Decide on a course of action.

A. Carefully define the problem.
B. List all the options or choices you can think of.
C. Rank these options in order of priority.
D. Select the option that you think is best and briefly discuss the probable consequences.

A Riot in the Making?

The correctional supervisor, Sergeant Jackson, is sitting in his cluttered, fly-specked office working a week-old crossword puzzle. Outside his window a black inmate in white coveralls fusses in the garden, snipping and raking, making sure that flower beds are just so. Across from the ''Visiting Park,'' other inmates march toward work areas. A prison runner jogs down the brick street inside the walls; the hundred-year-old live oaks that line the street stand motionless in the still afternoon heat. Elsewhere, the factory noises are beginning to resume following the noon break. The two-way radio crackles in Sgt. Jackson's office, but years of exposure to it have dulled his sensitivity and he no longer notices the radio except when it squawks for him.

This afternoon the Department of Corrections inspection team is scheduled to arrive. They will be accompanied by two newspaper reporters. An ad hoc group of professional and civilian members of the Governor's Prison Reform Committee has been touring the grounds for the past few days, surveying the more glaring inadequacies of the institution and suggesting remedies where possible. Several dormitory units have been quickly painted. Trash has been removed and burned, and there has been a general shakedown and cleanup of cellblocks. Even a new dinner menu has been created to provide more substantial and satisfying meals for the inmates.

The inmates are aware of the impending visit. Some of the more militant ones have been protesting the cleanup on the grounds that the administration is trying to cover up the inadequacies of the institution. Showers, which are usually allowed only twice weekly, have been increased to four times a week. Use of medication such as tranquilizers has been increased, and some of the inmates regarded as ''difficult'' have been removed to what is euphemistically called Administrative Segregation.

Even though Sgt. Jackson's office is less than a showplace, he has straightened it. His clipboard rosters and administrative directives, accumulated in reverse chronological order, hang from hooks instead of lying randomly on whatever flat spot that affords itself. Even as he works his crossword puzzle he keeps a government employee's wary lookout for premature or unexpected official visitors.

"Sgt. Jackson," the radio interrupts, "Sgt. Jackson."

The Sergeant reaches over, grabs the standing mike, and keys it. "Yeah, Jackson here."

"This is Tolliver. I've got the makings of a problem here. A group from 'E' wing has set up a committee and they want to speak, as a group, to the inspection team this afternoon. I told them I didn't think it was possible, but I said that I would ask you."

"Come on! You know that group of clowns; all they want is a country club. Troublemakers, every one of them. Tell them to forget it!"

"They are pretty insistent, sir."

"You make sure to remind them that the inspectors are only going to be here for a few hours, but we'll be here tomorrow, next week, and next year."

"Okay, I'll tell 'em."

Sergeant Jackson returned to his crossword puzzle, grumbling to himself about devious inmates always trying to get more than they deserved. Suddenly the radio came alive!

"Sergeant! Sergeant! A group of inmates are moving toward Central Control. They have pipes and appear to be holding three guards as hostages. Do you read?"

Sergeant Jackson grabbed the mike. "Yes, damn it. I read. How many are there? Exactly where are they? Do you have visual contact?" The voice on the other end failed to respond.

Sergeant Jackson looked up from his radio into the scowling faces of armed inmates. Central Control had been taken!

INSTRUCTIONS:

Decide on a course of action.

A. Carefully define the problem.
B. List all the options or choices you can think of.
C. Rank these options in order of priority.
D. Select the option that you think is best and briefly discuss the probable consequences.

A Question of Policy

A female correctional officer, you have been working at the same women's prison for fifteen years. The inmates call you Marge and respect you as being firm yet fair. You have made some mistakes during your career, but no one has ever questioned your intentions or integrity.

Like anyone working in a prison, you have found that there were some inmates you liked more than others. However, it is rare for you to find an inmate that you cannot work with at all. In fact, you are dedicated to the point that you will often spend some of your own time participating with the female inmates in recreation, arts and crafts, and other cellblock activities.

There is one inmate that you are particularly fond of. She is a young woman about nineteen years of age who is in on a drug offense. Lisa is a shy girl who comes from a broken home. She never had much of a family life; both of her parents had failed in previous marriages. Lisa's drug problems had started in high school when she got mixed up with the wrong crowd. She had felt acceptance by drug groups, and besides, life had seemed easier to cope with while on drugs. Lisa was just beginning to use hard drugs when she got busted. Because she was with a friend who was selling large quantities of drugs, her bust resulted in a trial and a two-year sentence.

While in prison, Lisa has come to you on several occasions with personal problems. Being a first time offender, she has found prison life very difficult to adjust to. You and she have become good friends in a mutually trusting relationship. On this particular day, however, your relationship has been tested.

Lisa has asked you to mail a personal letter to a close friend who lives in her home town. Since her friend is not a member of her family or her lawyer, his name is not on the approved mailing list. She knows your mailing the letter is a violation of institutional policy, but it is very important to her that she contact her friend just this one time. You know that other correctional officers occasionally mail letters for inmates. You also realize that it would be quite easy for you to mail this particular letter. Still, it is a violation of policy.

If you do not mail the letter, your and Lisa's relationship will more than likely deteriorate. If you do mail the letter, you may suffer unanticipated consequences. The decision is going to be a difficult one, and you are going to have to make it.

INSTRUCTIONS:

Decide on a course of action.

A. Carefully define the problem.
B. List all the options or choices you can think of.
C. Rank these options in order of priority.
D. Select the option that you think is best and briefly discuss the probable consequences.

Why Prisoners Riot

Vernon Fox, Ph.D.
Chairman, Department of Criminology,
Florida State University, Tallahassee

Finding valid, consistent, and reliable information as to why prisoners riot defies most standard methods of gathering data on human behavior. Official reports and most articles on the subject focus on overcrowding, poor administration, insufficient financial support, political interference, lack of professional leadership, ineffective or nonexistent treatment programs, disparities in sentencing, poor and unjust parole policies, enforced idleness of prisoners, obsolete physical plant, and a small group of hard-core and intractable prisoners.[1] Psychological viewpoints focus on aggression and acting-out personalities in the prison population.[2] Yet, while all the conditions mentioned in the sociological approaches exist in most prisons, the majority have not experienced riot. Further, all major prisons hold aggressive, hostile, and acting-out people. This leads to concern as to why these factors have been identified as causes of riot when riots have occurred in a small minority of prisons.

An examination of official reports following riots discloses a similar propensity for generalities and platitudes regarding causes of riots. These same conditions are consistently identified as causes of riots almost everywhere. The purpose of official reports, of course, is political in the sense that they give assurance to the general public after a riot that the remaining power structure in the prison has analyzed the causes, taken corrective measures, and merits the confidence of the public in that their interests will be protected. Investigating committees from governors' offices, legislatures, or other political directions seek simplistic answers that seem to structure their interpretations in accordance with the best interests of their own identifications. Reinterpretation of the situation has to occur frequently. Sometimes, the focus is on the predisposing causes, such as poor morale among inmates fostered by poor food or injudicious or misunderstood paroling policies. Sometimes, it is more aimed at the precipitating causes, such as a confrontation between an officer and some inmates. Sometimes, it has been explained as an attempted mass escape that the administration successfully contained.

Federal Probation, 35(March 1971), pp. 9-13. Reprinted by permission.

Many consultants who are invited from outside the jurisdiction as impartial experts tend to protect the person or group who invited them, which is ethical and logical. Diplomatic writing is a consultant's art. Other consultants invited from outside generally are not sufficiently well acquainted with the nuances and underlying intricacies of the power structure to understand as well as they might all the factors entering into a local situation. Whether the governor or the legislative committee chairman of an opposite political party was the source of the invitation seems to make a difference in the tone of the report. An impartial investigator must be aware of the political climate and what will and what will not be accepted in some political settings. Some reports have been rejected by political leaders, others have been used for political purposes, while many have just been shelved. In any case, the use of these reports for finding the real causes of riots must be tempered pending corroboration from other sources. Frequently, though, these reports may set the tone for further interpretation by the news media, political leaders, and writers of documentaries.

Identifying the causes of riot, then, is tenuous when official reports or statements *after* the riot are considered alone. Clearer vision can be obtained from news reports written *during* the riot. In decreasing order of validity and reliability, the materials that comprise this presentation are from (1) news stories during twenty serious riots since 1940 as reported in *The New York Times* during the action, (2) this writer's experience during the Michigan prison riot in 1952, (3) lengthy discussions with inmates involved in four prison riots, (4) conversations with prison personnel involved in seven prison riots, (5) literature concerning prison riots, (6) official reports and official statements *after* the riot, and (7) general literature on aggression, civil disturbances, and violence.

Causes must be divided into *predisposing* causes and *precipitating* causes. Just as in civil disobedience, there has to be a "readiness" to riot. Then, there has to be a "trigger." Too frequently, the predisposing causes have been used as causes for prison riots and the precipitating causes have been identified as causes for civil disorder. Neither is a cause, in itself. The total social situation, with emphasis on the interaction or lack of it between dominant people and subjugated people, either in the prison or in the ghetto, must be evaluated to determine why people riot. It cannot be based simplistically in overcrowding, political interference, lack of treatment programs, or any other simple answer.

PATTERNS OF RIOT

The way to make a bomb is to build a strong perimeter and generate pressure inside. Similarly, riots occur in prisons where oppressive pressures and demands are generated in the presence of strong custodial containment. Riots are reported more frequently from custodially oriented prisons. Even the riot in 1962 in the progressive and relatively relaxed District of Columbia Youth Center at Lorton, Virginia, involved suppression, real or imagined, of the Black Muslims.

Riots are spontaneous—not planned—detonated by a spontaneous event. The inmates know who has the weapons and who has the force. The inmates know that no administration ever has to negotiate with them. Planned disturbances end in sitdown strikes, slowdowns, hunger strikes, and self-inflicted injury. Escapes do not begin with disturbances unless they are planned as a distraction, though the disturbance may end in escape attempts. The spontaneous event that detonates the riot may be almost anything from a fight in the yard that expands, someone heaving a tray in the dining hall, to a homosexual tricking a new officer to open his cell, as happened in the Michigan riot in 1952. Violent riots must happen spontaneously. Otherwise, they would not happen. There has to be pressure, though, that builds up the predisposition or readiness to riot and a spontaneous precipitating event to trigger or detonate the riot.

Riots tend to pattern in five stages, four during the riot and one afterward. First, there is a period of undirected violence like the exploding bomb. Secondly, inmate leaders tend to emerge and organize around them a group of ringleaders who determine inmate policy during the riot. Thirdly, a period of interaction with prison authority, whether by negotiation or by force, assists in identifying the alternatives available for the resolution of the riot. Fourthly, the surrender of the inmates, whether by negotiation or by force, phases out the violent event. Fifthly, and most important from the political viewpoint, the investigations and administrative changes restore order and confidence in the remaining power structure by making "constructive changes" to regain administrative control and to rectify the undesirable situation that produced the riot.

The first stage of the riot is characterized by an event that triggered the unbridled violence. The first stage is disorganized among the prisoners and, too frequently, among the prison staff as well. It is at this point that custodial force could alter the course of the riot but, in most instances, custody is caught by surprise and without adequate preparation so that there is little or no custodial reaction other than containment. As a result, the riot pattern is permitted by default to move to the second stage.

The second stage is when inmate leaders emerge and the administrative forces become organized. Inmate leaders who emerge from this violence are people who remain emotionally detached sufficiently so that they lend stability to the inmate group. They "don't panic." They "keep their cool." As a result, they attract around them lesser inmate leaders or "ringleaders" who, similarly, do not panic but need to be dependent upon "the boss." In this manner, an inmate leader can gather around him probably two to six "lieutenants," each with some delegated authority, such as watching hostages, preparing demands, and maintaining discipline in the rest of the inmate group. Further, the inmate leader, like most political leaders, takes a "middle-of-the-road" position where he can moderate the extremes and maintain communication. In a prison riot, some inmates want to kill the hostages. Other inmates want to give up and surrender to the administration. The inmate leader controls these two extremes in a variety of ways and stabilizes the group into a position in the center.

The third stage is a period of interaction between inmates and prison officials. It has taken several forms, though they can be classified generally into (1) negotiation and (2) force or threat of force. No administration has to negotiate with prisoners, but the chances for negotiation are greater when the prisoners hold hostages. The chances for force or threat of force are greater when the prisoners do not have hostages. In either case, the decision on the part of the inmates to surrender is subject to the general principles of group dynamics. When the inmate group is cohesive and their morale is good, the prisoners will maintain the riot situation, whether faced with force or negotiaton. When the group cohesion begins to disintegrate by some inmates wanting to surrender, others wanting to retaliate, and the leadership wanting to maintain the status quo, the administration may manipulate it for an early surrender. This disintegration of group cohesion may be promoted by negotiation or by force or threat of force, depending upon the situation. In case of negotiation, the group cohesion is diminished by the administration's demonstrated willingness to negotiate and by the personality of the official negotiators who convey a feeling of trust and confidence. The group can be disintegrated, also, by gas, rifle fire, and artillery shelling, all of which have been used recently in American prison riots. The less destructive approach, of course, is to await disintegration of cohesion by periods of inaction that places strain to hold the group together on the leadership by fatigue and impatience. Faced with this situation, the leadership frequently has to look for an honorable way out of a disintegrating situation.

The fourth stage, or surrender, may be the inmates' giving up after being gassed and shot at or they may surrender in an orderly way either after force or threat of force or by negotiation. Political interference at the wrong time in the prison riot can affect the total situation in terms of negotiation, surrender, and subsequent investigations and administrative decisions.

The fifth stage, that of investigations, consolidation of the remaining power structure, personnel and policy changes followed by political fall-out, is really the most important stage, since it sets policy for the prison and the system for years to come. Editorials and news commentators suggest solutions and interpretations. Administrators have to respond satisfactorily to pressures from interest groups. This is why "get tough" policies become important after riots, even though they tend to intensify the problems.

Riots do not occur in prisons or correctional institutions with exceedingly high morale. Neither do they occur in prisons where the morale is so low that the prisoners endure penal oppression in a docile manner or break their own legs and cut their own heel tendons. Riots occur in prisons where inmates have medium to high morale and where some conflict appears in the staff, probably between treatment and custodial philosophies, and probably when the program is in a state of transition from one type of procedures and objectives to another.

Riots occur in prisons where there is a tenuous balance between controlling behavior and changing behavior. If there is a full commitment to either, riots do not occur. The riot itself, however, results in a political decision to *control* behavior. Consequently, the behavior changing in treatment forces always loses in a riot, at least in the immediate future.

There is also a direct relationship between news coverage by the mass media and the incidence of demonstrations, riots, and civil disturbances.[3] This is one reason why riots tend to cluster in terms of time.

One of the factors that contributed to the prison insurrections of 1952 was the decision of the administration to reverse the drift toward greater inmate control.[4] Abuses of official rules were curbed, preferential treatment for favored prisoners was eliminated, and the social system of the prison was "reformed" in the direction of the image of what the free community thought a maximum-security institution should be.

DURING THE RIOT

Guidelines for action during the riot are important. The custodial staff is frequently untrained and the administration is just as frequently caught by surprise. Action during the riot has to be planned ahead of time and modified according to the situation.

During the first stage of a riot, the disorganized inmates could well be effectively faced with force. As a matter of fact, most riots appear to have been vulnerable to custodial force in the early stages because of the disorganization on the side of the inmates. If disorganization occurs on both sides, however, then the riot cannot be contained early. Immediate custodial action could have altered the course of several riots. The lack of training, preparation, or even expectation of riot has resulted in disorganization on both sides for hours.

During the second stage, after the inmates have organized and their leadership begins to emerge, there is the question as to whether force should be used. No prison administration ever needs to negotiate with rioting prisoners. The prisoners know this. If hostages are held, then negotiation becomes a real possibility, depending upon other factors. If the inmates holding the hostages are young, reformatory-type people with short sentences and have not already demonstrated their capability to kill, if they are psychiatric patients who cannot organize into a team, or if their majority can see parole sometime in the future, then negotiation is not necessary. In the Michigan riot of 1952, the decision to negotiate was not made until after the files of the inmates holding the hostages in 15-block had been reviewed. In that situation, negotiation was apparently the only way to save the lives of the hostages. This was supported by subsequent reports by inmates, nationally known clinical psychologists, and consultants brought in for impartial investigation.

The third stage of the riot is determined by the nature of the situation. If no hostages are held or if the prisoners holding hostages are not hard-core intractables with nothing to lose, then force or threat of force is appropriate. If the hostages are considered to be in serious danger, the administration is placed in a real dilemma in determining action because lives have to be considered in relation to public and internal reaction and consequences. If waiting for fatigue to reduce the cohesion of the rebellious inmate group will accomplish the objective, then force is not necessary.

The fourth stage of the riot is the surrender. The regaining of custodial control is all that is needed. Any further action beyond the basic need has to be for public consumption or for the satisfaction of the prison administration.

The fifth stage of the riot is the aftermath where investigations, reinterpretations, and scapegoats are involved. There is not much the prison administration can do about this because the real power lies in the political structure. Free movement of newsmen and free access to information, both inmates and staff, is the only logical approach to take during this period. In this way, the administration can demonstrate that it is attempting to hide nothing, that it recognizes it has problems, and is openly and honestly seeking the best solutions.

In summary, official reaction to riot is dependent upon the situation. As in judo, the reaction is determined by the action of the adversary. No negotiation is needed where no hostages are held or where they might be held by short-term prisoners not considered to be dangerous. Out-waiting might be an approach in doubtful situations. An overshow of force is becoming decreasingly effective in American society and it invites unnecessary derision from some segments of the public.

ADMINISTRATIVE DOS AND DON'TS

Discretion, rather than negotiation or force, is at issue while handling a riot. A basic principle of police work or any other type of social control in a democratic society is to use the minimum amount of force and destruction needed to accomplish the objectives.[5]

Discretion is based on knowledge. Consequently, the first approach for a correctional administrator to improve his program is to increase the educational level of his staff by more selective recruitment and by inservice training. In modern democratic society, inservice training should be directed toward the social and behavioral sciences. This can be achieved by bringing neighboring junior colleges and universities into the educational program of the prison.[6] An understanding and knowledgeable prison staff from the custodial employee to the warden is important in the discretionary or decision-making process. It is this staff that determines whether a confrontation occurs or is avoided and, if it occurs, how it will be handled or accommodated. This is why they need to know social problems, personality development and problems, criminology and correctional procedures, as well as the law, particularly as it relates to civil rights.

The correctional officer is the key to riot prevention, although a rough and harsh custodial lieutenant, captain, or deputy warden can use policies and behavior to neutralize the good work of a hundred officers. The entire custodial force has to be treatment-oriented, just as the entire treatment staff has to be aware of custodial problems, in order to emerge with an effective correctional program.

Readiness to riot results from the predisposing causes, such as bad food, oppressive custodial discipline, sadistic staff quick to write disciplinary charges against inmates, and general punitive attitude by administration and line personnel. The precipitating cause that "triggers" the riot is very seldom the real cause. As previously mentioned, a bomb is made by constructing a strong perimeter or casing and generating pressure inside. It blows at its weakest point, but it has to be detonated. The detonation is not the "cause" of the explosion, although it "triggered" it.

During the riot, the inmates want to smash the system that keeps them hopeless, anonymous, and in despair, and they will destroy at random.[7] They become so alienated from society that they regard violence as right and proper. Good treatment programs and an accepting custodial staff tend to reduce this problem. A relaxed atmosphere in a prison that avoids this alienation is most important for the eventual correctional objective and to avoid riots.

How to achieve a relaxed atmosphere is sometimes difficult for the administrator because it appears that he is "taking sides." Custodial personnel are generally concerned with good discipline, which is sometimes interpreted as "nipping problems in the bud" and is translated into overreaction to minor offenses and oppressive custodial control. Many treatment personnel, on the other hand, are in a relaxed atmosphere because it tends to lower the inmates' defenses and permit casework and psychotherapy to be better achieved. The inmates, of course, find the relaxed atmosphere more comfortable, so they favor it. This places the treatment staff "on the side of the inmates," although for different reasons. It is sometimes difficult for an administrator to interpret to the custodial staff the reasons for promoting a relaxed atmosphere in the prison. This is another reason for providing education and inservice training in behavior and social problems to all staff.

Good food, plentiful and well prepared, is important to maintaining a prison. Napoleon's famous remark that an army marches on its stomach could be applied to any group of men. Food becomes a primary source of pleasure to men deprived of many of the comforts of normal life. Consequently, the prison administration cannot realistically compute food costs on the basis of nutritional needs alone. The emotional needs are important. An institutional program can make a lot of mistakes if it has a good kitchen that provides plenty of food. Conversely, food is a tangible item on which can be focused all the discontents and deprivations of the prison. Many riots have begun in or near the dining room. Food simply becomes a tangible substitute target for other complaints. Consequently, an administrator should spend a little extra time and effort to find a good steward to handle food services and pay special attention to the food budget.

Despite the other abuses, riots do not occur in prisons that are essentially run by inmates. There are some Southern prisons where selected inmates carry guns and guard other inmates. All the generalities attributed to riot causation exist, but no riots have occurred in these prisons. This is because the inmate leaders have a vested interest in the status quo and will protect it.

Inmate leadership is present in all prisons, as leadership is present in all groups of people. The constructive use of inmate leadership is an obvious way to avoid riots. Some type of inmate self-government that involves honest and well supervised elections of inmate representatives to discuss problems, make recommendations and, perhaps, even take some responsibilities from the administration could be helpful. Possibilities might be some control of those activities related to formalized inmate activities like manuscripts sent to potential publishers, pricing hobbycraft items for sale, or processing inmate activities like Alcoholics Anonymous or chess clubs. In an era when movements to unionize prisoners appear, such as in West Germany and Sweden, and when litigation initiated by inmates result in court rulings that change conditions and procedures within the prisons, it is the interest of the administration to know the inmates' thinking and their action. In any case, downward communication is not enough.

The pattern could be taken from student government functioning under a university administration. It could be taken from a civilian government operating under military occupation by the victors after a war, such as those civilian governments in Germany and Japan after World War II. The pattern in the Federal Bureau of Prisons and some other systems has been the inmate council, where elected inmates discuss problems and appropriate policies with the prison administration, making recommendations and suggestions. A suggestion box system for inmates might be instituted if other approaches appear to be too innovative. Regardless of how it is organized, it should promote upward and downward communication between inmates and prison administration and it should provide the inmate leadership with a vested interest in the status quo.

In summary, good communication can avoid the predisposing causes of riot. Whether by inmate council, inmate self-government programs, suggestion boxes, or free up-and-down communication of any type, knowledge by the inmate leadership of situations and their reasons can eliminate most predisposing causes. Establishment of the therapeutic community where inmates take responsibility for the improvement of other inmates, such as in the Provo Experiment in Utah in 1958-1964, the Minnesota State Training School at Red Wing, and some other places, would also provide a vested interest for the inmates in the institution and its program, as well as a constructive attitude. Raising the educational level of the prison staff, especially the correctional officers, would reduce the predisposing causes. Their better understanding of personality development and social problems would provide them with the capacity for discretion that would, in turn, reduce the precipitating causes. Prison riots can be eliminated when upward and downward communication, combined with discretionary use of authority, reduces the probability of serious confrontation that should not have to occur in a democratic society.

NOTES

1. A succinct and comprehensive review of the literature is found in Clarence Schrag, "The Sociology of Prison Riots," *Proceedings of the American Correctional Association, 1960,* New York, 1961, pp. 136-146.

2. For example, see the late Dr. Ralph Banay's excellent articles on causes of riots in *The New York Times,* July 26, 1959, sec. VI, p. 8: August 9, 1959, sec. VI, p. 2; August 16, 1959, sec. VI, p. 72.

3. David L. Lange, Robert K. Baker, and Sandra J. Ball, *Violence and the Media.* Washington, D.C.: United States Government Printing Office, November 1969, p. 614.

4. Gresham M. Sykes, *The Society of Captives.* Princeton, N.J.: Princeton University Press, 1958, p. 144.

5. See George E. Berkley, *The Democratic Policeman.* Boston: Beacon Press, 1969.

6. For suggested curricula, see Vernon Fox, *Guidelines for Correctional Programs in Community and Junior Colleges,* American Association of Junior Colleges, Washington, D.C., 1969, and "The University Curriculum in Corrections," *Federal Probation,* September 1959. Also see *Criminology and Corrections Programs,* Joint Commission on Correctional Manpower and Training, Washington, D.C., 1968.

7. "Violence and Corrections," *The Correctional Trainer,* Southern Illinois University, Carbondale, Vol. 1, No. 4, Spring 1970, pp. 56-91.

Social Climate and Prison Violence

Hans Toch, Ph.D.

*Professor of Psychology, School of Criminal Justice,
State University of New York, Albany*

There are two favored perspectives relating to prison violence. One—which appeals to would-be prognosticators (and to some wardens)—centers on *violent inmates*. This view has it that some inmates are consistently violent persons, who happen to be explosive in prison, but are likely to act out in almost any setting. A second portraiture conceives of inmate violence as at least partly a *prison product.* The most extreme version of this view is that of abolitionist critics who see prison aggression as a natural (and presumably, legitimate) reaction to the frustration of being locked up. Other critics also argue that prison incidents denote lax security, and thus suggest negligence. This view is to some extent shared by prison administrators, who think of controlling violence through perimeter architecture, ingenious hardware and deployment of custodial personnel. This context-centered view is a *negative* one, because it seeks to prevent violence by reducing the opportunities for aggression, rather than by trying to affect the motives and dispositions of violence participants.

In this article, I shall argue for a different context-centered view of prison violence which may offer more positive programming options than those that are conventionally envisaged. The view is also one that may have implications for research and policy.

THE ADVENT OF THE CONTEXTUAL VIEW

In the mid-sixties, the inmate-centered tradition was at its peak, and unusual prison incidents were viewed as correlates of offender background characteristics (MMPI profiles, prior criminality, etc.) with an eye toward locating high-risk offender groups.

Federal Probation, 42(1978), pp. 21-25. Reprinted by permission.

Among exceptions to this trend was a subgroup of The California Task Force to Study Violence in Prisons. In studying inmate aggression, this group partly focussed on the victimization *incident,* highlighting the immediate motives of inmate participants (aggressors and victims) that went into producing each incident (Mueller, Toch, and Molof, 1965). This sort of analysis illuminated (among other things) the contribution of extortion, homosexual relationships and pressures, debts, stealing, and routine prison disputes to the genesis of violent prison encounters in the mid-sixties.

This focus made possible a new approach to the motivational patterns of chronic, recurrent aggressors (in prison and outside prison), which dealt with trends in the way violent incidents arose for the same individual (Toch, 1969). This approach involved seeing violence precipitation as an intersection between violence prone personal dispositions and the situational stimuli that invoked these dispositions. In this view, a prison incident could result, for instance, given a perceived affront to an inmate who is oversensitive to such affronts, or from the availability of a tempting target to an inmate who is a habitual bully.

There are probably several ways of defining violence-relevant contextual stimuli such as the examples (peer challenges or vulnerable victims) we mentioned. One appealing term is "social climate" (Moos, 1974; Toch, 1977), because the concept of "climate" includes the inmate himself. In prison, the concern would be with each inmate's immediate world (staff, other inmates, physical setting) as the inmate experiences it and reacts to it. The presumption is that any prison setting in which inmates spend a significant portion of time (tiers, shops, classrooms, etc.) has behavior-relevant attributes that stand out for individual inmates. A shop, for instance, may feature a paternalistic foreman, relaxed (or firm) supervision, a group of street-raised youths (or lifers), high (or low) levels of noise, a playful (or businesslike) regime. Such factors may be more salient for most inmates than the fact that the shop teaches the plumbing trade, though this learning opportunity is another climate attribute that will be significant to inmates. Three fairly obvious points are of theoretical and practical concern: (1) any social climate feature may be critical in the life of one inmate and irrelevant to another; (2) the same feature may be welcomed by some and noxious to others, and (3) positive and negative reactions to features of climate helps motivate inmate behavior, including participation in violent incidents.

How do climate features enter into the genesis of violence? Consider the following examples, some of which are more complex than others:

(1) A farm setting in a youth prison is an informal haven for "problem" inmates because of its low level of supervision, which reduces the level of resentment and rebellious behavior; inmates who have been aggressors before arriving on this farm become relatively well-behaved; however, (a) an inexperienced rural inmate is assigned to the farm; he promptly becomes the target of homosexual pressure; (b) the victim evolves a panic reaction to the setting and the other inmates; in an effort at self-protection he assaults one of hs tormentors.

(2) A recreation room is popular on a tier because it offers opportunities for playful socializing; (a) recreational preferences develop into conflicts between two inmates, which produces a fight. (b) The incident participants are members of ethnic cliques, which become polarized and divide the recreation room into turfs; incidents arise as a result of jurisdictional disputes, and in retaliation for prior incidents.

(3) A prison is tightly supervised, except for certain areas in which an acknowledged need for privacy, or constant comings and goings, produce custodial lacuna; the places-and-times of low supervision acquire standard connotations; for instances: (a) the yard shower room is avoided by many inmates because it is frequented by sexual aggressors; a new inmate may wander into such an area. unaware, and become an incident victim; (b) a stairway used for movement from a tier to breakfast is comparatively unsupervised; it becomes a "gladiating arena" in which aggrieved inmates (some armed with knives) challenge their enemies; (c) in a tier with a tradition of informality, officers open gallery doors on request; the practice is abused by inmates wishing to invade the cells of fellow inmates to victimize them; (d) the inmate picnic becomes a drug-trafficking bazaar, with resulting jurisdictional disputes.

I have included examples in which traditional variables (particularly, the extent of supervision) play a role, but my implication is not that we must have 1984ish prisons in which monitoring is omnipresent. For one, custody is logically related to programming, and officers cannot be stationed where they are not otherwise needed, on the off-chance that incidents may occur. Deployment of security measures (whatever the level of security) of necessity must be uneven, leaving times and places of lower-density supervision. My point, in fact, is that neither custody deficits nor other formal arrangements of the environment produce violence. Incidents arise (as they do in the free world) because the relationships that spring up among people in a subsetting misfire or become sequentially destructive. There are chains of these motives, some of which get imported from outside the prison (such as the toughness-proving needs of our farm youths and the ethnic tensions in the recreational room). Personal motives get mobilized by environmental impingements, which press the relevant motivational button. Once a violence motive exists, meanings assigned to features of the environment (such as sex to the shower or gladiating to the stairway) then determine where and when incidents may occur.

SOCIAL CLIMATE AND AGGRESSORS' MOTIVES

I have implied that to understand incident motives in violence proneness means more than to locate prior behavior patterns or consistencies; it also means that we must know the stimuli that invoke the person's motives, the contexts that facilitate or invite them, the group that encourages or applauds them, and the milieu that makes them fashionable or susceptible to rationalization.

We must start with the incident; we ask ourselves how the victimizer arrived at his resolve. Was his goal profit? Retribution? Loyalty to his group? Wounded self-esteem? Search for reputation? Escape from danger? The temptation of another's vulnerability? Ethnic prejudice? Resentment of authority? Adherence to a "code"?

It is true that we can often infer the inmate's motives from his folder where the information we have about his prior behavior is richer than the data we have about victimization incidents; and it helps us differentiate *chronic* victimizers—whose personal behavior *patterns* must be addressed—from occasional victimizers, whose conduct is more of a product of specific situational forces.

But situational context is *always* of relevance—even with chronicity. A bully merits rehabilitative attention, but what such a person *immediately* needs is to be deprived of access to inmates with victim attributes. In a setting that is exclusively composed of self-styled "toughs" the predatory inmate's pattern is less likely to be elicited. Similar impact may be achieved by promoting solidarity among victim prone inmates (because bullies pick on isolates) or by promoting antibully norms among the bully's peers.

VIOLENCE PROMOTION BY CLIMATE FEATURES

Our point about situational context is not that the context *produces* the incident but that it *increases* or *reduces* the *probability* of incident occurrence. If our view holds, it follows that *incident prevalence can be increased or decreased through contextual interventions,* even though incident motives are personal and may be symptomatic of personality traits. Contextual facilitation of violence in prison occurs in several ways, some of the more obvious being:

(1) *By Providing "Pay Offs":* We can reinforce the motives of aggressors by conferring status or other types of rewards for violent behavior. In some cases the rewards are obvious, as when the aggressor secures peer admiration. Elsewhere there are more "hidden" reward systems, as when "punishment" consists of sending a predator to a status-conferring segregation setting.

(2) *By Providing Immunity or Protection:* Violence in prison benefits from the same "code of silence" that is highlighted by Westley (1970) for police violence; however the significance of the protective code in prison is compounded by inmate-staff social distance, by taboos against "ratting," by fear of retaliation, etc. Legalistic solutions to the victimization problem are encumbered by difficulties in securing reliable evidence, such as witnesses and victim-complainants. Prisons share this difficulty with other "subcultural" settings, such as those of organized crime.

(3) *By Providing Opportunities:* The prison world features predictability and routine, such as in physical movement, custodial supervison patterns, and types of staff reactions. The inmate aggressor is in the same position as the residential burglar who knows homeowner vacation patterns, and can plan time and locus of his victimization incidents. (Predictability, paradoxically, cuts both ways; by studying incident concentrations, we can readjust supervision patterns; staff readjustments can produce short-term amelioration, but must result in new incident clusters over time.)

(4) *By Providing Temptations, Challenges and Provocations:* Climate features may unwittingly or unavoidably contain stimuli that spark victimization, as does the "red flag" that mobilizes the bull. Prison juxtaposes "strong" and "weak" inmates, members of rival gangs, dealers and consumers of contraband, homosexual rivals, debtors and creditors, racketeers and "marks." Such stimuli are often "built into" population mixes, or into personal characteristics of inmates; others are "taken up" as optional roles. For instance, there are gangs that spring up in prison, in reaction to other indigenous inmate groupings—such as among Mexican-American

inmates in California. Prison gangs may engage in mutual retaliatory exercises in which each serves as the occasion for the other's violence.

(5) *By Providing Justificatory Premises:* Most inmates have more or less serious reservations about other inmates (Toch, 1977 a). The norm "never interfere with a (fellow) con" (Clemmer, 1958) includes a restricted range of select peers. Other fellow inmates may be (1) viewed as natural enemies or as personally contemptible; or (2) "dehumanized" to make them "fair game" for violence prone exploitation. If these considerations hold, controlling population mixes separates or combines potential aggressors, victims and violent contenders.

RESEARCH AND PROGRAM IMPLICATIONS

Prison outsiders have a penchant for outlandish recommendations. Worse still, they often ship coal (old ideas) to Newcastle. Some of my points will be familiar to prison staff; some suggest formalizing what is done, and affirming its value:

(1) *Understanding violence "hot spots" and low violence subenvironments:* Measures such as disciplining aggressors require little information about the causation of violence because the issue is culpability. Furthermore, incident participants are reticent in such inquiries, except for arguments in mitigation of their involvement. A corollary is that control and prevention of institutional violence cannot depend on information secured through fact-finding that occurs in disciplinary contexts.

I am not suggesting that formal research must be deployed in relation to violence, but that inquiries into the reasons for "cold" violent incidents (those no longer being processed) be undertaken. One form of such inquiry that strikes me as useful relates to settings in which violent incidents are generated, or where violence is scarce. (Parallel investigation can trace the institutional careers of violent inmates for "high points" and "low points" in their profiles.) Staff and inmates in violent subsettings—including incident participants—should be interviewed for clues about the high or low level of violence in their settings. Given everyone's stake in minimizing trouble, there is incentive for problem centered information sharing which has no disciplinary consequence.

Available statistics about unique subsettings (types of inmates, schedule of activities, levels of interaction, population movements, patterns of supervision) can be collated, and compared to (1) other subsettings, and (2) information about incident participants. Such data are merely *clues* to violence motives, but they serve to check (validate) data from interviews. Moreover, statistics "fed" to inmates and staff help them understand their violence problem.[1] This use is related to:

(2) *Helping inmates and staff in high violence settings address their own violence problem:* This gambit presumes that solutions that originate with those affected by their implementation are least likely to mobilize resistances. It also assumes that (as mentioned above) subsettings are communities that have a stake in reducing localized danger and disruption. The point holds even for violent individuals. Such persons have elsewhere become successfully engaged in "solving the violence problem" in their settings (Toch, Grant and Galvin, 1975). Staff and inmate groups can be run separately or together, charged with documenting the reasons for

violence patterns, and asked to recommend policy changes to neutralize violence patterns. This must obviously be done with the understanding that documented and practical suggestions will be implemented.

(3) *Creating Support Systems for Victims and Potential Victims:* Reactive violence measures address aggressors; by segregating them, they form prison enclaves (such as segregation wings) in which levels of violence become disproportionately high. Obvious victim centered strategies also entail problems. They stigmatize inmates (such as in "sissie companies") or may secrete prisoners in program voids, such as protective segregation areas. Less drastic options are available through the creation of new settings in which victim prone inmates are mixed with others, with clear programmatic purposes. Activity centered inmate groups in high violence settings can also provide victims with peer support and with respectable staff links.

(4) *Crisis Intervention Teams* are an example of support measures designed to be invoked where the violence problem is still "hot." One use of this strategy is the California deployment of inmate Social Catalysts (Sumner, 1976) who act as liaison and calming influences in gang wars, racial conflict and other group disturbances. Staff interventions can take forms counterpart to police family crisis teams, persons who are trained to defuse violent conflicts and who refer participants (if necessary) for professional assistance. Such teams can range in composition from chaplains to custodial officers or inmates. A less drastic option is to "debrief" violence participants (separately or in confrontation) to prevent lingering disputes from flaring up after the protagonists leave segregation and return to the yard.

(5) *Using Violence Related Data in Staff Training and Inmate Indoctrination* requires no technology beyond collation of relevant information. My suggestion is that such data should be as setting-specific as possible. In other words, the information would *not* consist of general "human relations" coursework for staff, or of rule centered, legalistic lectures to inmates, but of statistics and illustrations which sensitize staff and inmates to situations they are likely to encounter on the tier, on the job, in the classroom and in recreation areas. This means that "canned" curricula should be avoided in favor of updated information about contemporary interpersonal problems, group tensions, etc., and about solutions that have been tried and that have worked. Inmates and staff could also be specifically informed about the parameters of their assignments (informal routines, special population and their habits, etc.) so as to avoid dependence on scuttlebutt or trial and error learning.

None of these strategies will "solve" emerging problems. No matter what any of us do, low visibility disputes can arise and dedicated predators can find room for predation. The goal is the reduction of violence through the creation of a climate that faces occasions for violence and begins to defuse them. If we accomplish this goal, residual violence will be "person centered," and can be addressed as such.

REFERENCES

1. Clemmer, D. *The Prison Community.* New York: Holt, Rinehart and Winston, 1958.
2. Moos, R.H. *Evaluating Treatment Environments: A Social Ecological Approach.* New York: Wiley, 1974.

3. Mueller, P.F.C., Toch, H. and M.F. Molof. *Report to the Task Force to Study Violence in Prisons.* Sacramento: California Department of Corrections, August 1965.

4. Sumner, G.W. "Dealings with Prison Violence," in Cohen, A.K., Cole, G.F. and R.G. Baily (eds.) *Prison Violence.* Lexington, Mass.: D.C. Health (Lexington Books), 1976.

5. Toch, H. *Violent Men: An Inquiry into the Psychology of Violence.* Chicago: Aldine, 1968.

6. Toch, H. *Living in Prison: The Ecology of Survival.* New York: Free Press, 1977.

7. Toch, H., Grant, J.D. and R.T. Galvin. *Agents of Change: A Study in Police Reform.* Cambridge, Mass.: Schenkman (Halsted/Wiley), 1975.

8. Westley, W.A. *Violence and the Police: A Sociological Study of Law, Custom and Morality.* Boston: M.I.T. Press, 1970.

NOTES

1. One use of data feedback relates to fear of violence (secondary victimization), a topic I have not touched upon because it deserves detailed rumination. Fear relates *imperfectly* to violence, and this means that we may be afraid without cause, or unafraid where apprehension might well be functional. Information about violence that *does* occur in a setting can be a corrective to irrational apprehension. Similarly, fear can be separately mapped, and such data can be discussed as a direct effort at fear reduction or fear alignment.

Selected Bibliography

ANKERSMIT, EDITH. "Setting the Contract in Probation," *Federal Probation,* 40(1976):28–33.

BRODSKY, STANLEY L. "A Bill of Rights For the Correctional Officer." *Federal Probation,* 38(1974):38–40.

BRASWELL, MICHAEL. "The Problem Inmate: An Adjustment Process." *The Southern Journal of Educational Research,* 8(1974):292–300.

CARROLL, LEO. *Hacks, Blacks and Cons: Race Relations in a Maximum Security Prison.* Lexington, Massachusetts: Lexington Books, 1974.

HARTINGER, WALTER. *Corrections: A Component of the Criminal Justice System.* Santa Monica, Calif.: Goodyear Publishing Co., 1973.

HORNE, ARTHUR M. and PASSMORE, J. LAWRENCE. "Inservice Training in a Correctional Setting." *Federal Probation,* 41(1979):35–39.

JACOBS, JAMES B., and GROTTY, NORMA M. *Guard Unions and the Future of Prisons.* Ithaca, N.Y.: New York State School of Industrial and Labor Relations, Cornell University, 1978.

JOHNSON, ROBERT. "Informal Helping Networks in Prison: The Shape of Grass-Roots Correctional Intervention." *Journal of Criminal Justice,* 7(1979):53–71.

KATSAMPES, PAUL. "Changing Correction Officers: A Demonstration Study." International Journal of Criminology and Penology, 3(1975):42–45.

MCNAMARA, CHARLES. "Killing of a Correctional Officer and His Family Prompts Colorado to Move Out on Tough Legislation." *American Journal of Corrections,* 38(1976):26–27.

STATSKY, WILLIAM P. "Teaching Corrections Law to Corrections Personnel." *Federal Probation,* 37(1973):42–47.

WICKS, ROBERT J. "Is the Corrections Officer a Second Class Citizen?" *American Journal of Corrections*, 36(1974):32–36.

WITTMER, JOE; LANIER, JAMES E.; and PARKER, MAX. "Race Relations Training With Correctional Officers." *The Personnel and Guidance Journal*, 54(1976):302–306.

THE COUNSELOR

Correctional counselors deal with the emotional climate of a correctional environment, attempting to provide inmates with adjustment and rehabilitation counseling services. These services may be rendered on an individual basis or in a group setting.

The following seven cases and reading will present you with a variety of professional and personal situations correctional counselors typically find themselves in. Dealing with inmate depression, anger, and deception, as well as with the counselor's own sense of frustration are examples of functions required of the correctional counselor. As you react to the cases, consider the feelings of the counselor and the inmate with which he or she is working.

A reading on the application of reality therapy with offenders is included at the end of the section.

Wet Behind the Ears

Four years at the university studying corrections and sociology have finally paid off. You have landed your first job, as a correctional counselor in a medium-sized prison. Although you do not have any previous work experience, you were an "A" and "B" student in school and did especially well in correctional theory. After arranging your new office to your taste and lighting up your newly purchased pipe, you prepared yourself for becoming a dynamic part of the rehabilitation process.

At the beginning of the work day you met with the other counselors and your supervisor for coffee and the day's caseload assignments. You were somewhat puzzled at the mixture of amused and disinterested stories that greeted your remarks on the latest research and theory concerning the practice of correctional counseling. As the day wore on you became even more perplexed. The security officers escorting your inmate clients were always at least fifteen minutes late. Two of your clients did not even come for counseling; one, who was illiterate, wanted you to read a letter for him from home, and another one wanted you to help him complete some kind of "leather work" kit order form. To make matters worse, you noticed that two of the other counselors worked with only one client each during the entire morning, while you took care of four different clients. The two counselors spent most of their morning drinking coffee and "shooting the breeze" with each other in one of the offices.

After lunch everything seemed to slow down even more. You could not even get one of your scheduled clients in to see you at all. When you discussed the problem with the security officer responsible for escorting your client, he turned to you with a sneer and replied, "I got more important things to do than to escort convicts all day." Then without another word, he abruptly walked away before you even had a chance to reply.

You carefully related to your supervisor everything you had observed that day, giving special attention to the insulting security officer. You had liked your supervisor from the start and you knew he would quickly straighten this whole mess out. Perhaps that is why you were so shocked when his only response was that you were new on the job and that you needed to "take it easy."

The end of your first working week finds you tired and confused. None of the other counselors seem to care about rehabilitation or any of the other things they were taught in college. They all have behavioral science degrees. What has happened to them? Will the same happen to you? Your supervisor told you to take it easy and give the others a chance to get to know you. Was your initial positive impression about him wrong? Is a career in corrections right for you, or was your choice a mistake?

INSTRUCTIONS:

Decide on a course of action.

A. Carefully define the problem.
B. List all the options or choices you can think of.
C. Rank these options in order of priority.
D. Select the option that you think is best and briefly discuss the probable consequences.

Confidentiality or Security?

You have been working as a counselor at the community correctional center for three years. You feel good about your job and the results you have achieved. No inmate or civilian has ever questioned Tom Brown's ethics or integrity.

You are presently working on an especially interesting case. A young twenty-two-year-old second-time drug offender named Ted has really been opening up to you and seems to be turning himself around in terms of his personal values and motivation. The trust between the two of you is apparent. In fact, just several days ago the superintendent commented on how better your client seemed to be doing since you had taken him on your caseload. However, during the last counseling session your client disclosed something that could severely disrupt your relationship with him and you are not sure what to do about it.

Halfway through your last session, in a moment of frustration, Ted blurted the whole thing out. Apparently he and two other inmates had been planning an escape for some time. After Ted became your client and began making progress, he began to have second thoughts about being involved in the escape. The other two inmates, however, threatened to implicate him if anything went wrong with their attempt. The escape attempt is planned for the following night. Ted is distraught as to what he should do, and since you are his counselor, you are somewhat distraught also.

As a correctional counselor you are not only responsible for counseling inmates, but have implicit security responsibilities as well.

If the escape attempt is allowed to continue as planned, correctional officers, inmates, or both might be seriously injured or killed. If the plan is quashed, you will have failed to honor the confidentiality of your client, and Ted will most probably suffer repercussions. Needless to say, your counseling relationship with him will also be severely damaged.

It seems you have to either sacrifice Ted and your counseling relationship with him or the security of the correctional center. Confidentiality or security, which must it be? Can there be another way?

INSTRUCTIONS:

Decide on a course of action.

A. Carefully define the problem.
B. List all the options or choices you can think of.
C. Rank these options in order of priority.
D. Select the option that you think is best and briefly discuss the probable consequences.

Conning the Counselor

You have been working with Willie for six months now and he has made excellent progress. Willie is an old "con" who has been in prison for some time. In fact, he has served a total of fourteen of his fifty-five years behind bars. In the beginning he had very little use for the counseling or educational programs your department offered. On several occasions he was approached concerning his learning to read and write but had become insulted and stalked away.

You gradually got to know Willie through your mutual interest in sports. Willie was a walking encyclopedia of sports information. There was not a player in professional baseball whose strengths and weaknesses and, of course, batting average, Willie did not know. Willie also had an uncanny knack for successfully predicting the outcome of professional and collegiate sports events. One day when the two of you had been mulling over the latest sports news, you had mentioned to Willie that he ought to write a sports column for the prison newspaper. As soon as you brought the subject up, you remembered that Willie could not read or write. You prepared yourself for a negative outburst from him, but none ever came. Instead, several days later he walked into your department and announced that he wanted to learn to read and write so that he could, indeed, write a sports column. Now it is six months later and he has made excellent progress—until today.

A few minutes ago Sergeant Howard informed you that Willie had established a drug pick-up in the library during the extra study time you had granted him. In fact, Willie and several of his cohorts had been caught by security officers in the library with contraband drugs in their possession. They had been placed in administrative segregation while awaiting formal charges. The sergeant's parting words were still ringing in your ears: "I told you; you can't trust convicts. They will only use you."

Needless to say, you are disappointed and hurt that Willie has abused his relationship with you. Being exploited never feels good, but it will be especially embarrassing for you because of the jokes the security officers are sure to make about how you were "taken in." Yet the fact remains that Willie had made progress. Had his only motive been the drugs, or did he really want to write that sports column? How should you react to him when he comes back to the cellhouse? Should he be allowed to continue his basic education, or should his access to the prison school and library be terminated?

INSTRUCTIONS:

Decide on a course of action.

A. Carefully define the problem.
B. List all the options or choices you can think of.
C. Rank these options in order of priority.
D. Select the option that you think is best and briefly discuss the probable consequences.

What's the Use?

You have been a caseworker at the state prison for five years. During that time you have written up case reports on hundreds of inmates. Although each inmate's file contained other important information such as psychological, educational, and aptitude test results, you had always felt the case report was the most valuable indicator of an inmate's adjustment and rehabilitation potential. With the aid of various test results, background information, and other relevant material, the experienced caseworker can, in one interview, integrate all the information into a meaningful perspective describing the offender's adjustment to prison and receptiveness to treatment and rehabilitation programs. You had always said, "One good caseworker can give a more accurate picture of where an inmate's head is in a one-hour interview than all the test results a psychologist can put together."

However, as committed as you are to that notion, lately you have begun to wonder why you are going to so much trouble with your reports. Some of the older caseworkers have told you all along that the administration was not really concerned with the quality of the case reports, but just wanted something in the inmate's files to cover themselves in the event something happened. You are beginning to believe them, especially since learning that the assistant warden has automatically been including a statement in each psychological evaluation that the inmate is an "escape risk," just in case the inmate did ever attempt to escape.

Even more distressing is your growing realization that the case reports are usually referred to only after some harmful event such as a suicide attempt or physical assault. Very rarely is case report information used to place an offender in particular counseling, vocational, or educational programs. Your case reports always seemed to be utilized after the fact.

You do not want to become like the older caseworkers who are resigned and bitter concerning their work, yet you are finding it increasingly difficult to feel good abut what you are doing. You have considered several options, among them discussing the problem with the warden, initiating an "evaluation team" approach that would include security officers, and just generally trying to revive the sagging spirits of the other caseworkers. You are not sure what you should do, but you realize you need to do something if you are to continue feeling good about working as a correctional caseworker.

INSTRUCTIONS:

Decide on a course of action.

- A. Carefully define the problem.
- B. List all the options or choices you can think of.
- C. Rank these options in order of priority.
- D. Select the option that you think is best and briefly discuss the probable consequences.

The Group

Ever since you earned your master's degree in social work, you have focused your counseling interests and skills on the group process. You have even had a couple of articles published describing your group counseling efforts at the community-based halfway house where you are presently employed. Group work, in your opinion, is the best way to help people solve their problems. It is economical and efficient; you can see ten clients in a group during an hour, while in individual counseling you can see only one person at a time. Of course, you realize that individual counseling is necessary at times. Nevertheless, the group approach is usually better because it requires the group members to interact with each other rather than only with the counselor.

You have utilized the "encounter" group process quite effectively on several occasions in the past with juvenile drug offenders. Confrontation seems to be particularly effective in dealing with the "conning" behaviors of many drug users. This approach also seems well suited to your personality as a therapist; no one has ever accused you of being nonassertive when dealing with a client.

Your most recent group, however, is proving to be a perplexing and frustrating experience. What began as a typical group of juvenile offenders engaged in open confrontation has degenerated into intimidation and thinly disguised threats. You have even heard rumors that some threats are being made outside the group. You realize you are losing control of the group, but are not sure what to do about it. You have confronted the group several times recently regarding their intimidation and lack of basic respect for each other. Despite your reprimands, the sessions are becoming more destructive. You could terminate the group meetings, but you hate to admit defeat, especially since you have never had to terminate a group in the past. You continue to rack your brain for a solution to your group's lack of progress. There has to be an answer somewhere.

INSTRUCTIONS:

Decide on a course of action.

- A. Carefully define the problem.
- B. List all the options or choices you can think of.
- C. Rank these options in order of priority.
- D. Select the option that you think is best and briefly discuss the probable consequences.

The Despairing Client

John has been in prison for two years. He is a likable inmate who works in the prison library. Usually quiet, John has a remarkable talent for repairing damaged books. He has saved the library hundreds of dollars by his handiwork.

As his counselor, you try to see him at least once a month to find out how he is getting along. He always indicates that he is doing all right and that he is optimistic regarding his parole hearing which is only nine months away. John has some reason to feel good about his chances for making parole. He is a first-time offender who got into a drunken brawl at a tavern and seriously injured another man. As a result of the altercation, he was sentenced to six years in the state penitentiary. Although John had experienced severe drinking problems for a number of years, fighting had never been a part of the problem. Since being in prison, he has joined Alcoholics Anonymous and has even successfully completed several college level courses in library science. Needless to say, counseling John is a pleasant experience mostly because of his own motivation.

However, in the last several weeks John's behavior and attitude have changed. His wife, who has been visiting him faithfully every Sunday, has not shown up for the last two visitation days. Cellhouse rumor is that she has begun seeing another man and is planning to file for a divorce. To make matters worse, the man she is involved with is an alcoholic himself. John has quit coming to work and stays to himself in the cellhouse. He has also been losing weight and looks haggard and distraught.

As his counselor you want to help, but John, who has always been quiet, has now become even more withdrawn. You are not sure how to approach him. You have considered talking to his wife or his parents. If John's depression continues to worsen, his behavior may become unpredictable. He might become aggressive and get into a fight with someone in the cellhouse or he might turn his anger inward and attempt suicide. You have to approach him, but how? You have to do something in an attempt to help him, but what?

INSTRUCTIONS:

Decide on a course of action.

   A. Carefully define the problem.
   B. List all the options or choices you can think of.
   C. Rank these options in order of priority.
   D. Select the option that you think is best and briefly discuss the probable consequences.

Dealing with Anger

You have been a counselor for ten years, but this is one part of your job that has never gotten any easier.

Doug, an inmate at the institution where you work, has just been turned down for parole for the second time in six years. The two of you are sitting at the hearing room table silently staring out the barred window. You can see the tears silently streaming down Doug's face. You can sense the anger and humiliation he is feeling and the explosion within himself that he is fighting to contain.

Doug has a good prison record with respect to both his conduct and his commitment to rehabilitation programs. The problem is apparently a political one. The local judge simply does not want Doug released in his county. As the institutional counselor, you know several other inmates who have been granted parole to that particular county. They were paroled despite their having committed more serious offenses than Doug and having been much less receptive to the various institutional rehabilitation programs. Doug also knows of these paroles. To make matters worse, the parole board did not even give him a reason for rejecting his application, nor did they tell him what he could do to increase his chances for parole.

Doug spent weeks in preparation for his parole hearing. The letters of recommendation, the acquisition of his high school diploma, and other related material had in the end meant nothing. The board had convened less than ten minutes to make a parole decision based on six years of Doug's life. The chairman simply told you that Doug's parole had been denied and for you to pass the decision along to Doug. You had reluctantly done so, knowing that Doug could see the decision in your eyes before you even spoke. So here the two of you sit, bitter and dillusioned.

Will Doug give up? Will his anger get him into trouble with the administration or other inmates in the cellhouse? How will this affect your relationship with him, since you were the one who encouraged him to apply? You are not sure what to do or say, but somehow you have to try to help Doug pick up the pieces.

INSTRUCTIONS:

Decide on a course of action.

A. Carefully define the problem.
B. List all the options or choices you can think of.
C. Rank these options in order of priority.
D. Select the option that you think is best and briefly discuss the probable consequences.

Reality Therapy: Helping People Help Themselves

Richard L. Rachin
Chief, Bureau of Group Treatment
Florida Division of Youth Services
Editor, Journal of Drug Issues

Efforts to redirect the behavior of persons who violate laws, customs, and morals are often unsuccessful, perhaps because we tend to view behavior different from our own as evidence of mental illness of some kind or degree. We ignore legal, cultural, and other idiosyncratic determinants of who may be "okay" today and who may be in trouble tomorrow, and instead seek pathological explanations for nonconforming behavior. Many people have been harmed by our insistence that human behavior is understandable and thereby treatable only in terms of mental health or mental illness, a dogma that has compartmentalized, isolated, and stigmatized those who, for one reason or another, act unconventionally. This paper explores a more humanistic, economic, and societally productive alternative for changing behavior and considers its application and availability to offender groups in particular. Reality therapy departs radically from the conventional treatment orthodoxy. The conceptual differences between the two approaches as well as the basic steps for practicing reality therapy are also outlined and discussed.

The realities of mental-health operations, said Anthony Graziano two years ago, "seldom match the idealism with which they are described in the rhetoric."

Our professional rhetoric is powerfully reinforcing when it enables us to obscure our own doubts and to disguise our own shortcomings. We seldom actually do what we say we are really doing. Sustained by their own deception, individual clinicians believe they are performing noble functions in essentially bureaucratic, unsympathetic, and doubtfully effective agencies.[1]

Reprinted, with permission of the National Council on Crime and Delinquency, from Richard L. Rachin, "Reality Therapy: Helping People Help Themselves," *Crime and Delinquency,* January 1974, pp. 45-53.

Graziano was not saying anything new. This same message has been delivered, with increasing volume, since the early fifties. Only recently, however, have the efficacy and ethical underpinning of classical treatment procedures been openly attacked.[2] Today it seems almost fashionable to expose, if not castigate, psychoanalysts for defects of character and purpose—faults which they have always shared with the rest of us.[3]

While psychotherapy, particularly of the psychoanalytic type, has never proven to be more effective or dependable than less pretentious kinds of help, orthodox practitioners tend to be as defensive as shamans in examining this incongruity. With certain notable exceptions, there is a remarkable absence of discussion among psychotherapists concerning the efficacy of their treatment techniques in spite of the paucity of evidence mustered to support the belief that psychotherapy is more effective than other treatment procedures.

The influence of mental health practitioners is largely responsible for acceptance of the view that socially disapproved behavior is evidence of emotional illness. Too often the label becomes a self-fulfilling prophecy building impenetrable barriers between *them* (those labeled) and the rest of us.

People in trouble, whether they are patients in mental institutions, drug dependents, or kids who play truant, often are not in a position where they can choose to be treated or not be treated. Public agencies armed with clinical evaluations make the choice for them. The recipient of such public largesse and his family have had little to say about rejecting or terminating treatment, even when the service seems to endanger his health and well-being.[4] Explanations designed to justify these practices are patronizing and lack the evidence that would support continuing them.

Ponder Graziano's theme that American mental health practitioners seem more concerned about improving their status and enhancing their power base than they are about treating. Clinical services have not been freely available to persons needing such care—especially in correction, where both the quality and the quantity of clinical personnel have left something to be desired. Considering juvenile correction alone, the President's Crime Commission reported that, of the 21,000 persons employed during 1965 in 220 state-operated juvenile facilities, only 1,154 were treatment staff. While the accepted national standard required one psychiatrist for every 150 juvenile inmates, the actual ratio in American institutions for children was 1:910. Forty-six psychiatrists (over half of them concentrated in five states) were then listed as the treatment backbone of juvenile correction.[5] As Donald Cressey observed, "The trap is this: We subscribe to a theory of rehabilitation that can be implemented only by highly educated, 'professionally trained' persons, and then scream that there are not enough of these persons to man our correctional agencies and institutions."[6]

DISSATISFACTION WITH THE MEDICAL MODEL

The following are some of the reasons for the accelerating development of alternatives to traditional, medically based approaches to helping troubled people:

    1. "The recidivism rate for offenders," writes Seymour Halleck, "remains

depressingly high and the number of psychiatrists interested in treating the delinquent remains shamefully low."[7] Publicity given to crime and the problems of our criminal justice system has not led to any significant increase in the numberof clinicians devoting themselves to correction.

2. Even if there were enough conventionally prepared clinicians available, it is doubtful that government would be able or willing to assume the cost of their employment. Psychiatric attention is expensive and psychiatry's patients in the correctional system have never been high on the list of public priorities.

3. Important class, cultural, and racial barriers between those treating and those being treated have hindered the development of rapport and effective treatment programs. This problem has been magnified by our dependence on institutional care and the location of most of the institutions in rural areas, where staff recruitment beyond the surrounding communities (when attempted) is usually unsuccessful. Generally, in a state with a relatively large urban population, few of the staff—but, conversely, a disproportionately large part of the inmate population—are members of city-dwelling minority groups.

4. Research has not demonstrated that people receiving conventional treatment are any better off than those not receiving treatment. While this may be disturbing to advocates of the status quo, it is well to recall Jerome Frank's words: "Comparison of the effects of psychotherapy and placebos on a group of psychiatric outpatients suggest certain symptoms may be relieved equally well by both forms of treatment and raises the possibility that one of the features accounting for some of the success of all forms of psychotherapy is their ability to arouse the patient's expectation of help."[8] We are witnessing an accelerating growth of more humane, socially accountable therapies in which people with problems depend on other people with similar problems for help. The influence that human beings have on one another has long been noted, but has not been applied in practice.[9]

Although middle-class values and standards provide no valid measure for assessing mental health or mental illness, this yardstick has been customarily employed to measure deviation and the need for correctional care, especially in juvenile courts. Fortunately, simple economics has forced a reexamination of the traditional treatment orthodoxy. We have finally come to question the concept of mental illness as behavior that deviates from an established norm and its concept of cure as intervention by professionally trained mental health practitioners.

There should be little argument about the pervasive long-term ineffectiveness of most "treatment" programs. Although poorly trained staff, crumbling and inadequate physical plants, skimpy budgets, and overcrowding contribute to their futility, it is doubtful that unlimited resources alone would make it possible to rehabilitate significantly more offenders. Many private child-care agencies with budgets and per capita costs several times those of their public counterparts have discovered this when they become involved with court-referred children—even though they have been highly selective when deciding which court-committed children they will accept. A major reason for the poor results may be that many of the ways in which most well-adjusted adults once behaved are now viewed as symptomatic of underlying pathology. Two important circumstances are usually overlooked: (1) usually behavior brought to the attention of the courts and other official agencies is disproportionately that of poor and minority group children; (2) as George Vold observed, "in a delinquency area, delinquency is the normal response of the normal individual. . . . The nondelinquent is really the 'problem case,' the nonconformist whose behavior needs to be accounted for."[10]

The imprimatur of the court clinician is usually sufficient to dispose of children whose true feelings and needs are probably better known to their peers than to anyone coming into contact with the child for the first time. As Martin Silver found, "The detection of a 'proclivity to bad behavior' is facilitated by the court's 'treatment' process." Silver goes on to quote Dick Gregory: "Being black is not needing a psychiatrist to tell you what's bugging you."[11]

Offenders who have proved to be poor candidates for traditional treatment approaches in many cases seem responsive to peer group "here and now" therapies. As Carl Rogers expressed it, "It makes me realize what incredible potential for helping resides in the ordinary untrained person, if only he feels the freedom to use it."[12] The medical model for understanding and treating essentially psychosocial, ethical, or legal deviations makes it, as Szasz suggests, "logically absurd to expect that it will help solve problems whose very existence has been defined and established on nonmedical grounds."[13]

Nevertheless, when available in correction and more than just in name, diagnostic and treatment services essentially remain cast from the same orthodox mold. Vested interests and ignorance combine to apply a method of treatment that even Freud himself was to disavow in later life.[14] Ironically, proposals made to improve treatment services are usually accompanied by pleas for more psychiatrists, clinical psychologists, and psychiatric social workers. The influence which mental health practitioners have had on the design and delivery of treatment services seems accounted for not by any greater success in helping people but by seemingly convincing arguments disparaging alternative approaches. Put to the test, conventional treatment practices based upon the mental health/mental illness model have been as unsuccessful with offender groups as they often have been unavailable. Operating in the penumbra of the clinician and frequently in awe of him, legislators and correctional administrators have clung tenaciously to procedures about which they understand little and feel the need to understand less. And this problem has not been restricted to correction.

The development of less costly, more effective, and readily attainable treatment alternatives can be traced to three conditions: first, a quest for involvement, understanding, and clear communication by significant numbers of people—a need which could hardly be met by the small coterie of conventional mental health practitioners; second, voluntary patients' dissatisfaction with the time and expense required for treatment; and third, a crescendo of criticism directed by practitioners and researchers at a treatment methodology that has never been validated.[15]

William Glasser shared this concern. Near the completion of his psychiatric training he began to doubt much of what he had been taught. "Only a very few questioned the basic tenets of conventional psychiatry. One of these few was my last teacher, Dr. G. L. Harrington. When I hesitatingly expressed my own concern, he reached across the desk, shook my hand and said 'join the club.'"[16]

REALITY THERAPY

Glasser's theories departed radically from classical procedures. He postulated that, regardless of the symptom—be it drug use, fear of heights, suspicion that others may be plotting against one, or whatever—the problem could be traced in all instances to an inability to fulfill two basic needs:

> Psychiatry must be concerned with two basic psychological needs: *the need to love and be loved and the need to feel that we are worthwhile to ourselves and to others.* [17]

Glasser believed that the severity of the symptom reflected the degree to which the person was failing to meet these needs. No matter how bizarre or irrational the behavior seems to be, it always has meaning to the person: a rather ineffective but nevertheless necessary attempt to satisfy these basic needs.

Regardless of behavior, people who are not meeting their needs refuse to acknowledge the reality of the world in which they live. This becomes more apparent with each successive failure to gain relatedness and respect. Reality therapy mobilizes its efforts toward helping a person accept reality and aims to help him meet his needs within its confines.

We fulfill our needs by being involved with other people. Involvement, of course, means a great deal more than simply being with other people. It is a reciprocal relationship of care and concern. Most people usually experience this relationship with parents, spouses, close friends, or others. When there is no involvement with at least one other human being, reality begins to be denied and the ability to meet one's needs suffers accordingly.

Glasser points out that advice given to a person who needs help is of little value. People who deny the reality of the world around them cannot be expected to respond to exhortations to do better or to behave. Involvement means having a relationship with another person who can both model and mirror reality. The reality therapist presumes that people who are experiencing difficulty in living are having difficulty meeting their needs within the confines of the "real world." To help someone adopt a more successful life style, the reality therapist must first become involved with him. Involvement is the reality therapist's expression of genuine care and concern. It is the key to his success in influencing behavior. Involvement does not come easily. The therapist must be patient and determined not to reject the person because of aberrance or misbehavior.

REALITY AND TRADITIONAL THERAPY COMPARED

Reality therapy rejects the classical system whereby problem-ridden people are viewed as mentally ill and their behavior is labeled according to a complex and extensive classification scheme. Instead of the terms "mental health" and "mental illness," reality therapy refers to behavior as "responsible" or "irresponsible." The extensive, ambiguous, and unreliable diagnostic scheme on which conventional practitioners depend is discarded. As diagnostician the reality therapist simply determines whether the person is meeting his needs in a manner that does not interfere with others meeting theirs. If he is, he is acting responsibly; if he isn't. he is acting irresponsibly.

Conventional procedures lead the patient back through a maze of old experiences in search of the origin of his problem, because, the analyst assumes, the patient will be unable to deal with the present until he understands how the problem began in the elusive link in the past. Reality therapy concentrates on the present, on the "here and now" rather than the "there and then." Nothing can change the past, no matter how sad or unfortunate it may have been. The past does not influence present behavior any more than the person permits it to. The focus of the reality therapist, therefore, is on present behavior, about which something can be done.

Conventional therapy emphasizes the process during which the patient relives significant occurrences in his past and projects his past wishes, thoughts, and feelings onto the therapist; through interpretation of these past events the therapist helps the patient understand his present inadequate behavior. In contrast, reality therapy rejects the need for insight into one's past; the reality therapist relates to the person as he is and does not relive the past. The conventional practitioner seeks to uncover unconscious conflicts and motivations and to help the patient gain insight into these mental processes; he deemphasizes conscious problems while helping the patient understand his unconscious through dreams, free associations, and analysis of the transference. The reality therapist insists that the person examine his conscious self and behavior; conceding that efforts to understand motivation or other complex mental processes may be interesting, he doubts that the results merit the time spent to obtain them: it has yet to be demonstrated, he argues, that these pursuits have anything to do with helping the person.

Conventional practice makes no ethical judgments and frees the patient of moral responsibility for his actions; it views the patient as being under the influence of a psychic illness which makes him incapable of controlling his behavior. In reality therapy the patient is forced to face the consequences of his behavior: Was it right or wrong? What were the results for him?

Finally, the conventionally schooled practitioner insists that his role remain inexplicit, almost ambiguous, to the patient; he does not take an active part in helping him find a more productive way to live. Although the reality therapist does not take over for the person, he helps him—even teaches him when necessary—to learn better ways to meet his needs.

FOURTEEN STEPS

The reality therapist follows certain steps in attaining involvement and influencing responsible, realistic behavior. Responsibility, the basic concept of reality therapy, is defined simply as the ability to meet one's needs without depriving others of the ability to meet theirs. Realistic behavior occurs when one considers and compares the immediate and remote consequences of his actions.

Step 1: *Personalizes.* The reality therapist becomes emotionally involved. He carefully models responsibility and does not practice something other than he preaches. He is a warm, tough, interested, and sensitive human being who genuinely gives a damn—and demonstrates it.

Step 2: *Reveals Self.* He has frailties as well as strengths and does not need to project an image of omniscience or omnipotence. If he is asked personal questions he sees nothing wrong with responding.

Step 3: *Concentrates on the "Here and Now."* He is concerned only with behavior that can be tested by reality. The only problems or issues that can be confronted are those occurring in the present. Permitting the person to dwell on the past is a waste of time. He does not allow the person to use the unfavorable past as a justification of irresponsible action in the present.

Step 4: *Emphasizes Behavior.* Unlike attitudes or motives, behavior can be observed. The reality therapist is not interested in uncovering underlying motivations or drives; rather, he concentrates on helping the person act in a manner that will help him meet his needs responsibly. Although the person may be convinced that new behavior will not attain responsible ends, the reality therapist insists that he try.

Step 5: *Rarely Asks Why.* He is concerned with helping the person understand what he is doing, what he has accomplished, what he is learning from his behavior, and whether he could do better than he is doing now. Asking the person the reasons for his actions implies that they make a difference. The reality therapist takes a posture that irresponsible behavior is just that, regardless of the reasons. He is not interested in time-consuming and often counterproductive explanations for self-defeating behavior. Rather, he conveys to the person that more responsible behavior will be expected.

Step 6: *Helps the Person Evaluate His Behavior.* He is persistent in guiding the person to explore his actions for signs of irresponsible, unrealistic behavior. He does not permit the person to deny the importance of difficult things he would like to do. He repeatedly asks the person what his current behavior is accomplishing and whether it is meeting his needs.

Step 7: *Helps Him Develop a Better Plan for Future Behavior.* By questioning *what* the person is doing now and *what* he can do differently, he conveys his belief in the person's ability to behave responsibly. If the person cannot develop his own plan for future action, the reality therapist will help him develop one. Once the plan is worked out, a contract is drawn up and signed by the person and the reality therapist. It is a minimum plan for behaving differently in matters in which the person admits he has acted irresponsibly. If the contract is broken, a new one is designed and agreed upon. If a contract is honored, a new one with tasks more closely attuned to the person's ability is designed. Plans are made for the contract to be reviewed periodically.

Step 8: *Rejects Excuses.* He does not encourage searching for reasons to justify irresponsible behavior: to do so would support a belief that the person has acceptable reasons for not doing what he had agreed was within his capabilities. Excuses do not improve a situation; they do not help a person to see the need for an honest, scrutinizing examination of his behavior. Excuses only delay improvement.

Step 9: *Offers No Tears of Sympathy.* Sympathy does little more than convey the therapist's lack of confidence in the person's ability to act more responsibly. The reality therapist does not become inveigled into listening to long sad stories about a person's past. The past cannot justify present irresponsible behavior. The therapist has a relationship with the person which is based upon genuine care and concern; sympathizing with a person's misery or inability to act in a more productive and need-fulfilling manner will do nothing to improve his ability to lead a responsible life. The therapist must convey to the person that he cares enough about him that, if need be, he will try to force him to act more responsibly.

Step 10: *Praises and Approves Responsible Behavior.* People need recognition and esteem for their positive accomplishments. However, the reality therapist should not become unduly excited about a person's success in grappling with problems that he previously avoided or handled poorly. But just as a person's irresponsible behavior is recognized when he is asked what he plans to do about it, so should his responsible behavior be recognized.

Step 11: *Believes People Are Capable of Changing Their Behavior.* Positive expectations do much to enhance the chances of a person's adopting a more productive life style regardless of how many times he may have failed in the past. Negative expectations, on the other hand, serve to undermine progress. It is easier to do things well when others are encouraging and optimistic.

Step 12: *Tries to Work in Groups.* People are most responsive to the influence and pressure of their peers. It is much easier to express oneself with a group of peers than it is to relate to a therapist alone. People are also more likely to be open and honest with a peer group. Problems one often imagines are unique are quickly discovered by group members to be similar to the difficulties others also are encountering. Group involvement itself is immediate and helpful grist for observation and discussion. Learning experiences derived from interaction in treatment groups carry over to personal encounters.

Step 13: *Does Not Give Up.* The reality therapist rejects the idea that anyone is unable to learn how to live a more productive and responsible life. There are instances when a person may be unwilling to do anything about his life, but this does not mean that, given another opportunity, he will not work to change it. Failure need not be documented in a detailed case record. Case records too often become little more than repetitive and largely subjective harbingers of failure. Sometimes professionals seem more involved with records than with the people the records pretend to describe. The reality therapist does not let historical material interfere with his becoming involved with people or prevent him from beginning afresh.

Step 14: *Does Not Label People.* He does not believe that elaborate diagnostic rituals aid involvement or help the person. Behavior is simply described as responsible or irresponsible. The therapist does not classify people as sick, disturbed, or emotionally disabled.

The principles of reality therapy are common sense interwoven with a firm belief in the dignity of man and his ability to improve his lot. Its value is twofold: it is a means by which people can help one another, and it is a treatment technique, applicable regardless of symptomatology. It is simple to learn albeit somewhat difficult for the novice to practice. Experience, not extensive theoretical grooming, is the key to accomplishment.

Correctional clients who have proven least amenable to conventional treatment methods respond well to reality therapy. That its employment involves only a fraction of the time as well as the cost required by traditional (and not more effective) psychoanalytically oriented treatment modalities only further underscores its value. Until research can demonstrate its relative effectiveness and permanence, these reasons alone make its utilization well worth a try.

NOTES

1. Anthony M. Graziano, "Stimulus/Response: In the Mental-Health Industry, Illness Is Our Most Important Product," *Psychology Today,* January 1972, p. 17.

2. *Los Angeles Times,* June 26, 1972, p. 3.

3. Phyllis Chester, "The Sensuous Psychiatrists," *New York,* June 19, 1972, pp. 52-61.

4. Frontal lobotomy, electric shock, and insulin therapy to relieve anxiety were far from being the most humane procedures. See Percival Bailey, "The Great Psychiatric Revolution," *American Journal of Psychiatry,* 113(1956):387-406. Those who have complete confidence in the new wonder drugs should see Richard Elman's "All the Thorazine You Can Drink at Bellevue," *New York,* Nov. 22, 1971, pp. 40-46; also, *New York Times,* July 15, 1972, p. 7.

5. President's Commission on Law Enforcement and Administration of Justice, *Task Force Report: Corrections* (Washington, D.C.: Government Printing Office, 1967), p. 145.

6. Donald R. Cressey, remarks on "The Division of Correctional Labor," in *Manpower and Training for Corrections,* Proceedings of an Arden House Conference, June 24-26, 1964, p. 56.

7. Seymour L. Halleck, "The Criminal's Problem with Psychiatry," *Morality and Mental Health,* eds. O. Hobart Mowrer et al. (Chicago: Rand McNally, 1967), p. 86.

8. Jerome D. Frank, *Persuasion and Healing* (New York: Schocken Books, 1964), p. 74. See also R. G. Appel et al., "Prognosis in Psychiatry," *A.M.A. Arch. Neurol. Psychiat.,* 70(1953):459-68; O. H. Mowrer, *The Crisis in Psychiatry and Religion* (Princeton, N.J.: Van Nostrand, 1961), p. 121; Hans D. Eysenck, *The Effects of Psychotherapy* (New York: International Science Press, 1966), p. 121.

9. J. Dejerine and E. Gauckler, *The Psychoneuroses and Their Treatment* (Philadelphia: J. B. Lippincott, 1913), p. 17.

10. F. Lovell Bixby and Lloyd W. McCorkle, "Discussion of Guided Group Interaction and Correctional Work," *American Sociological Review,* August 1951, p. 460.

11. Martin T. Silver, "The New York City Family Court: A Law Guardian's Overview," *Crime and Delinquency,* January 1972, p. 95.

12. Carl Rogers, *Carl Rogers on Encounter Groups* (New York: Harper & Row, 1970), p. 58.

13. Thomas S. Szasz, "The Myth of Mental Illness," *American Psychologist,* 15, (1960).

14. J. Wortis, *Fragments of an Analysis with Freud* (New York: Simon and Schuster, 1954), p. 57.

15. Eysenck, *Effects of Psychotherapy,* p. 94; quotes D. H. Malan, the Senior Hospital Medical Officer at London's Tavistock Clinic, the locus of orthodox psychoanalysis in England: "There is not the slightest indication from the published figures that psychotherapy has any value at all."

16. William M. Glasser, *Reality Therapy: A New Approach to Psychiatry* (New York: Harper and Row, 1965), p. xxiii.

17. Ibid., p. 9.

Selected Bibliography

ALONZO, THOMAS, and BRASWELL, MICHAEL. "Behavior Modification and Corrections: An Analysis." *L.A.E. Journal,* 40(1977):10–16.

BENNETT, LAWRENCE; ROSENBAUM, THOMAS; and MCCULLOUGH, WAYNE. *Counseling In Correctional Environments.* New York: Human Services Press, 1978.

CHANELES, SOL. "Prisoners Can Be Rehabilitated—Now." *Psychology Today,* October, 1976, pp. 129–134.

COOKE, GERALD. "The Behavioral Treatment of the Rapist." *Prison Journal,* 58(1978):47–52.

DAVIS, DUANE; STURGIS, DANIEL; and BRASWELL, MICHAEL. "Effects of Systematic Human Relations Training on Inmate Participants." *Rehabilitation Counseling Bulletin,* 20(1976):105–109.

EHRENWALD, JAN. *The History of Psychotherapy.* New York: Jason Aronson, 1976.

FROMM, ERICH. *Man for Himself.* New York: Holt, Rinehart and Winston, 1947.

GENTHNER, ROBERT W. and HART, SUSAN. "Three Psychotherapy Systems and Their Facilitation of Personal Responsibility." *Journal of Humanics,* 5(1977):46–53.

GLASSER, WILLIAM. *Reality Therapy.* New York: Harper and Row, 1965.

GOLDMAN, JANICE G. "The Female Psychologist in an All-Male Correctional Institution in Philadelphia." *International Journal of Offender Therapy and Comparative Criminology,* 20(1976):221–224.

HIPPCHEN, LEONARD J. *Correctional Classification and Treatment.* Cincinnati: W. H. Anderson Company, 1975.

JAMES, MURIEL. *Born to Love.* Reading, Mass.: Addison-Wesley, 1973.

KASLOW, FLORENCE W. "Marital or Family Therapy for Prisoners and Their Spouses or Families." *Prison Journal* 58(1978):53–59.

KEEN, SAM. *Voices and Visions,* New York: Harper and Row, 1970.

LIPTON, DOUGLAS; MARTINSON, ROBERT; and WILKS, JUDITH. *The Effectiveness of Correctional Treatment: A Survey of Treatment Evaluation Studies*. New York: Praeger, 1975.

MAHRER, ALVIN R., and PEARSON, LEONARD. *Creative Developments in Psychotherapy*. New York: Jason Aronson, 1973.

PATTERSON, G.R. *Families: Applications of Social Learning to Family Life*. Research Press Company, 1971.

PEOPLES, EDWARD E. *Readings in Correctional Casework and Counseling*. Santa Monica, Calif.: Goodyear Publishing Co., 1975.

PONZO, ZANDER. "Integrating Techniques from Five Counseling Theories." *The Personnel and Guidance Journal*, 54(1976):414–410.

SZASZ, THOMAS S. *The Age of Madness*. New York: Jason Aronson, 1974.

WARNATH, CHARLES F., and SHELTON, JOHN L. "The Ultimate Disappointment: The Burned-Out Counselor." *The Personnel and Guidance Journal*, 55(1976):172–175.

WATTS, ALAN W. *Psychotherapy East and West*. New York: Pantheon Books, 1961.

WILKS, JUDITH, and MARTINSON, ROBERT. "Is the Treatment of Criminal Offenders Really Necessary?" *Federal Probation*, 40(1976):3–9.

WILSON, G. TERRANCE, and DAVISON, GERALD C. "Behavor Therapy: A Road to Self-Control." *Psychology Today*, October, 1975, pp. 54–60.

THE CORRECTIONAL ADMINISTRATOR

The effective correctional administrator, whether in a community or a more traditional institutional setting, must be a person who possesses significant management and interpersonal skills.

The seven cases and the reading in this section will provide you with a sampling of what problems you might expect as a correctional administrator. Being a female superintendent of a women's prison, dealing with political pressures from within and without the correctional agency, attempting to solve the problems of prison sexuality, and handling a disturbance where inmates have taken a hostage are some of the problem situations you will be given to react to in this section.

A reading on practical research suggestions for correctional administrators is included at the end of the section.

Anyone Want a Job?

You have been chairperson of the State Board of Corrections for three years now and the situation has never been more perplexing. You and the board members must find a competent commissioner for the Department of Corrections, and no one who is well qualified seems to be interested in the job. Correctional Administrators, especially at the top level, always seem to come and go with some degree of regularity, but the situation in your state is getting to be ridiculous.

Two years ago the governor pushed the corrections board for a new professional administrator, one who could, as the governor put it, "show us the light at the end of the tunnel." Jim Plant, who had run afoul of the federal courts, decided conveniently to resign, and Dr. Ron Hatch was hired from a progressive western system. After stormy confirmation hearings, Hatch and the staff he had brought with him fell victims to the devices of certain political pressure groups that had backed the newly elected governor. The corrections board eventually requested and received Dr. Hatch's resignation. A temporary commissioner, Gil Swanson, was appointed, but he was uneasy and unenthusiastic about his appointment and really did not want the position permanently. Gil had retired from the federal system and had no intention of entering a political "hot bed" for any extended period. He contended that the salary of thirty-six-thousand dollars a year was not worth a heart attack or a nervous breakdown.

Nevertheless, the glitter of a powerful bureaucratic position was difficult to reject, and Swanson assumed the role of the caretaker of the status quo, while the corrections board tried to locate and recruit a suitable administrator. Since there was no one in the state who could satisfy all the political factions, the search centered around out-of-state candidates, for whom, according to statute, minimum qualifications were "a masters degree in the field plus a minimum of five years' full-time experience in corrections."

When Hayward Adams, a well-known and aggressive administrator, applied, everyone was pleasantly surprised. Adams had a fine record and was a smooth political in-fighter. Best of all, he was a thorough professional and could probably provide the first innovative leadership the state's correctional system had ever had.

Adams's entry into the system made everyone happy, even the politicians who for fifty years had considered the prison system as a political pork barrel. Commissioner Adams took the reins of an archaic system and with amazing coolness and singleness of purpose, he began putting together progressive programs and weeding out ineffective staff members and fruitless programs. There was no doubt that a professional was at work.

Problems soon began to develop, however, as the weeding out process began to take its toll of political "spoilers," while some of the administration's most outspoken critics were retained. In one day, Adams received five calls from the governor's office interceding in personnel actions. The final blow was when Adams's choice for deputy commissioner was blocked by an emissary from the governor's office, who proclaimed the selectee was on the wrong side of the political fence and could not be trusted.

Adams felt that this intrusion into his management prerogatives was unwarranted and was destructive of his ability to manage the system. As unexpectedly as Adams appeared on the scene, he resigned after only six months on the job and took a position on a Presidential Advisory Board. A stunned public was aghast at the developments, and legislators were vocal in their criticism of the governor and his staff, but the damage was done and for the fourth time in two years the state was seeking someone to head the Department of Corrections.

Henry Harris, a newcomer to the state system, has applied for the vacant position, but his education is less than required by statute. Despite his good track record as an institutional administrator, the legislature is not likely to amend the statute to accommodate his employment. In addition, Harris has rejected the suggestion that he return to school to meet the degree requirements, but he does still want the job.

Dr. Frank Reynolds, a criminology professor at the state university who has some work experience in correctional settings and considerable administrative experience in the criminal justice field, has been rumored to be a possible candidate. He has held several high level state appointments in the state criminal justice system and seems to get along well with politicians and the correctional staff, but Dr. Reynolds has privately said he would not be interested in the job. Nonetheless, since he does meet statutory requirements, he is still being considered.

Norman Smith, Director of the Juvenile Services Divsion, is a capable person who has about ten years' experience in Juvenile Corrections and meets the educational requirements. He is skeptical about the future of any new adult corrections commissioner in the state and enjoys the security of his present position, despite the fact that the new position would afford him a substantial pay raise. Norman might be convinced, but right now he is not applying. He has a good job.

As chairperson of the Board you want to "get the ball rolling" towards selection of a new corrections commissioner—one that will stay. The question is where do you begin?

INSTRUCTIONS:

Decide on a course of action.

- A. Carefully define the problem.
- B. List all the options or choices you can think of.
- C. Rank these options in order of priority.
- D. Select the option that you think is best and briefly discuss the probable consequences.

Who's Running the Prison?

You came to the state correctional system with good credentials; an ex-military officer whose fifteen years in high level correctional management positions and recent completed masters degree in Criminal Justice seemed to prepare you for almost any correctional-related position. You have a practical, no-nonsense attitude and feel quite comfortable in being appointed superintendent of the state penitentiary, which had been suffering from incompetent leadership and political intrigue.

The facility was in the state's most isolated corner, and the inmates there were either considered to have little potential for rehabilitation or were serving such long-term sentences that rehabilitation was of little immediate interest. In accepting the job as superintendent, you stated that your top priorities were to upgrade conditions in the prison, especially the physical plant, and to improve the quality of the correctional officer staff. Recently the two problems have become entwined in an unexpected way.

You had only been on the job for one week when the county commissioner for the district in which your institution is located came to see you. The commissioner, as you soon learned, was a political power in the county and could make conditions miserable for you if he wanted. It seems that his son-in-law needed a job and he wanted you to find a place for him on your staff. One word led to another and before you knew it you responded by stating, "Hell no! I won't hire anybody unless they are qualified." The county commissioner left angrily, and a day later Senator Nester called. Senator Nester was on the state corrections committee and represented the district in which your institution was located. At the time he called you did not know that he was also on the appropriations committee. You learned later that if someone wanted a management job at the institution, he had to call

Senator Nester in order to be hired. Senator Nester stated in his call to you that he just wanted to "get acquainted" and give you a little friendly advice. First, he indicated that you should make a serious effort to get along with all the local officials, and second, he recommended that you hire the county commissioner's son-in-law. You told the senator that you would look at the son-in-law's application when he submitted it, and if he was qualified, you would give him serious consideration, but beyond that you could make no promises.

Your review of the son-in-law's hastily submitted application revealed that he had a high school diploma, had been a police officer on a local force, and had several other unrelated jobs all of rather short duration. In short, he might be qualified for an entry level correctional officer slot. However, his work record was spotty and the reason for his departure from the police department was unclear. Although no one was talking openly about it, there were some allegations of police brutality involving the son-in-law circulating from certain members of the department. Since you did not want an unqualified and questionable political hack in your organization, you placed his application in "file 13."

After a week Senator Nester's office called "on behalf of a constituent" and inquired about the son-in-law's application. Your personnel officer told the senator's office that a letter had been sent to the applicant thanking him for his application, but informing him that applications were competitive and, unfortunately, he had not been selected.

Later in the day Senator Nester called back in person; he was enraged. "Why wasn't I informed of the turn down? I've done a hell of a lot for this correctional system, and have a right to expect the courtesy of a reply. I never had this problem before." Nester was clearly threatening when he said, "You may find that these upcoming hearings will question your practices in dealing with the legislature, and I'll have some questions about your personnel policies, too." You finally told Senator Nester that you were running the institution, and until you were replaced you would continue to hire people based on merit.

Two months later at budget hearings in the legislature, you found out Senator Nester was a man of his word. Because of his influence, a new car for the prison superintendent was stricken, slots for eighteen new correctional officers were also stricken, and to make matters worse, the committee voted to nullify the badly needed pay raises that had been budgeted for all the prison employees.

The senator's message has come through to you "loud and clear." You realize that the two of you will have to reach some sort of working agreement, unless you can marshall enough support from other more friendly legislators, which at present does not seem likely. The question for you now is: how should you approach Senator Nester? How can you maintain your standards and at the same time appease him? Should you give and take a little, should you look for a new job, or should you do both? You are not a quitter; you would prefer to work with Senator Nester, but you keep asking yourself how.

INSTRUCTIONS:

Decide on a course of action.

A. Carefully define the problem.
B. List all the options or choices you can think of.
C. Rank these options in order of priority.
D. Select the option that you think is best and briefly discuss the probable consequences.

A Hostage Has Been Taken!

The situation at the state prison had been getting progressively worse for several months. Since there were very few jobs, the majority of the inmates had been idle. Because of a cutback in the budget, education and recreation programs were almost nonexistent. As the newest and youngest warden of a state penitentiary in your state, you had inherited a deteriorating situation, to say the least.

The grumbling had continued to grow louder and louder from the cellblocks until the anger erupted. A cellhouse officer had engaged in a confrontation with a group of inmates concerning their lack of respect for the officers and prison administration. A heated argument had followed, and the officer, who was alone in the cell block, was prevented from leaving the area. A hostage was taken! The inmates then informed the warden via the prison intercom system that they had a list of demands that had to be met if the correctional officer was to remain unharmed.

The list of inmate demands included everything from a new recreation gym to extra rations of smoking tobacco. Although many of the demands were impossible, some, such as the extra tobacco and longer recreation periods, could, with relatively minor difficulty, be accommodated. But even if some concessions were made, the hostage's safety would still be in question. The officer had been informed when he was hired, as all prison employees are, that there were risks in prison work—including being taken hostage. In addition, the official policy of the State Department of Corrections was that no negotiating with inmate groups could be conducted while they held hostages.

You are being pressured to make a decision. The Chief of Security wants to move quickly with his riot squad, hoping to catch the inmates by surprise and quell the disturbance before the hostage can be seriously injured. Although you agree with him emotionally, there seem to be too many "ifs" in his plan. The family and friends of the hostage are urging you to negotiate with the inmates. The press wants an interview. You have to make a decision and stand behind it firmly. What will you do?

INSTRUCTIONS:

Decide on a course of action.

A. Carefully define the problem.

B. List all the options or choices you can think of.

C. Rank these options in order of priority.

D. Select the option that you think is best and briefly discuss the probable consequences.

Prison Sexuality

You have been Superintendent of the State Adult Correctional Facility for six months. Having worked in the field of corrections for over ten years, you have developed quite a list of improvements you would like to implement. These changes include a number of areas in Security and Treatment.

You can remember when you started out your correctional career as a Security Officer. After years, you were promoted to a Security Supervisor. Years later you transferred into the counseling department as a Counselor III. Your transfer coincided with your graduation from a nearby university which you had been attending part-time for a number of years. With your newly earned Master's degree in Correctional Counseling, you attempted to strengthen your institution's treatment program, particularly in the area of Crisis Intervention, and had achieved some degree of success with your efforts. In your most recent position, you served successfully as an Assistant Superintendent at a smaller medium security institution.

As Superintendent you methodically worked with your list of improvements. It is six months later, and you have come to item number four, "How to deal effectively with the problems of prison sexuality, particularly sexual assault."

Sexual assaults by aggressive older male inmates against younger prisoners has continued to increase at the prison. It is one thing to tolerate homosexual relationships between consenting adults, but quite another to deal with the young and sometimes older victims of homosexual rape. Of all the difficult situations you have found yourself in as a prison administrator, the most difficult by far have been the times you have had to face the rape victims. Depressed, humiliated, and emotionally torn apart, they looked to you as a correctional administrator for help;

as usual, there was little solace you could give them. Sure, you could transfer them to another prison or place them in administrative segregation, but that would provide only a partial solution. You could never guarantee them that they would not be attacked again. They knew what the situation was and, as a result, usually refused to identify their assailants out of fear of an even worse attack as retaliation.

There are a number of theories concerning the best way to handle sexual problems in prison. A well-respected colleague of yours isolated all admitted homosexuals in a single cellblock. Another superintendent housed all suspected aggressive homosexuals in a special prison camp, and other correctional administrators tried to segregate all potential rape victims from the general inmate population. Each of these approaches has positive and negative qualities and you are not sure which one is best. Your particular prison houses between one thousand and one thousand and five hundred adult male inmates age eighteen and older. Your institution, which was built in the late 1930s, averages between forty and fifty serious sexual assaults each year which are reported or confirmed by correctional offiers. Of course, there is no way to know how many assaults actually occur, since many go unreported. You are not sure which approach is most effective, but as Prison Superintendent you intend to take the lead in developing a strategy to deal with sexual problems in your prison.

INSTRUCTIONS:

Decide on a course of action.

  A. Carefully define the problem.
  B. List all the options or choices you can think of.
  C. Rank these options in order of priority.
  D. Select the option that you think is best and briefly discuss the probable consequences.

Managing a Women's Prison

You are the new Superintendent at the State Adult Women's Prison. No one had believed you would continue working toward a career in correctional administration. Even your husband, a physician, had from time to time doubted the value of your efforts. You persevered, and now, in your mid-thirties and after nine years of marriage, a career, and two children, you have been appointed Superintendent.

After your first tour of the institution, you were somewhat disheartened. The drab green paint was peeling off the walls. The prison library consisted of sixty or so books and a ragged set of encyclopedias. The recreation room was poorly stocked with damaged equipment from the men's prison. The faces of the women pretty much reflected their environment and the winter season—depressed.

Your first objective was to remodel the facility, if painting the walls and repairing the heating system could be considered remodeling. In any event, two coats of paint and a new heating system later, the place at least looked more cheerful.

The administrative problems facing you were numerous and immense. The prison needed increased treatment, vocational, and educational programs; improved health care; additional facility renovations and additions; improvement in food preparation and quality; more effective prison security; and additional correctional personnel. Correcting the deficiencies in the women's prison would require not only sophisticated management skills, but a substantially increased operating budget as well. The State Commissioner's initial response to your budget request was not very supportive. Since women inmates comprise only 10 percent of the state's incarcerated adult offenders, the Commissioner was reluctant to allocate funds he felt could be better utilized elsewhere.

You could not help feeling that his reluctance stems at least in part from his being a man; you feel that he does not give the women's prison the consideration it deserves because he is not aware of the needs of women. How could a man fully understand the special needs of female offenders? Somehow you have to help him become more aware of the female offender. Even if you can gain some budget increases, that will probably not be enough. Community resources may also be available if you can motivate local business and civic leaders. Being a female superintendent of a women's prison has proven to be as much of a challenge as you thought it would. Changes need to be made. You have the will and now must find the way.

INSTRUCTIONS:

Decide on a course of action.

A. Carefully define the problem.
B. List all the options or choices you can think of.
C. Rank these options in order of priority.
D. Select the option that you think is the best and briefly discuss the probable consequences.

Businessperson or Correctional Administrator?

The need for some type of halfway house for juveniles who needed supervision and guidance rather than incarceration was apparent to officials in the juvenile court and to most of the community leaders. Many juvenile offenders had been sent to the state training school because there were no residential facilities in the community. Far more had been released outright when it became apparent that there was no appropriate facility for them. Usually a grandparent on social security or an older sibling provided the alternative residence.

You are an intake counselor in the youth court and felt something must be done. Accordingly, you discussed the problem with your regional supervisor and decided that the best tactic was to approach a certain civic organization. The group you chose is composed of young, progressive businesspeople in the community who are active in developing innovative social programs. They already had a national crime prevention program and you felt your ideas might fit in.

Your discussions with the group proved fruitful; they agreed to give support in the form of cash contributions, services, and item donations. However, it was left to you to locate the facility. Although real estate is not one of your strengths, you did hear that an old home was willed to a church under conditions that prevent its sale, and it was deteriorating from lack of use. The minister of the church agreed to lease it to you for one dollar per year, if you would agree to cover all maintenance costs. While the house is not ideally located, it is close enough to schools and accessible to public transportation.

A call for old household furnishings was placed in the weekly bulletins of two large churches and brought more than an adequate response. Within a short time there was enough furniture to open the halfway house. Some renovation was still necessary, however. An electrical contractor in the civic group agreed to make the necessary repairs on the electrical system. When it became evident that a new water heater was also needed, a friend of yours who is a plumber agreed to supply the labor if you could find a gas water heater. A local hardware merchant came to your rescue. Finally, the facility was livable!

The next question to be resolved was that of a house director and counselor. The city fathers asked you to be the house director and also agreed to a salary of $850.00 per month for a qualified live-in husband and wife team to manage certain aspects of the facility, counsel, and supervise the juveniles living there. After an extensive search you were able to recruit a young doctoral student in counseling psychology and her husband. The county, in exchange for joint use of the facility, agreed to pay $10.00 per day for each juvenile remanded there. With civic donations continuing to dribble in and a modest government grant, you felt that you had developed a respectable alternative to the state training school.

The first six months of operation were very successful, especially from the standpoint of the twelve juveniles who were living there. There have been no incidents among the residents; all are in school, and if there is a visible problem, it is only that the facility should be larger.

Toward the end of the first year's operation, however, some problems began to surface. There was an unpaid $380.00 telephone bill that was incurred by one of the residents. There was a nasty rumor circulating that the counselor's husband was more "fatherly" with some of the girl residents than a houseparent should be. Worst of all, funds which were thought adequate for the year were depleted, with necessary expenses far exceeding expected income.

You decided to bring your plight to the attention of the county commissioners. They quickly informed you that there was no more money in the budget. You received the same response from the city fathers. The business community was appalled by what they felt was a lack of financial management in dealing with the budget. A local realtor who was spearheading your community fund-raising efforts through various businesses told you that "the well had run dry," and that there had been an implicit expectation that the residence center would be properly managed. Furthermore, you were notified that until you could devise some scheme to pinpoint financial responsibility and dispel the unsettling rumors of sexual exploitation by a certain staff member, there would be no more support from civic groups or members of the business community.

You are faced with a variety of immediate and serious problems, including the possible reduction of your resident population, possible dismissal of the residential counselor and her husband, and the demise of the only juvenile diversion project in the county. You are about ready to give up. You want to find a way to salvage the halfway house project, but you cannot seem to come up with any viable answers. You are beginning to wonder whether you should have majored in business administration in college instead of corrections.

INSTRUCTIONS:

Decide on a course of action.

A. Carefully define the problem.

B. List all the options or choices you can think of.

C. Rank these options in order of priority.

D. Select the option that you think is best and briefly discuss the probable consequences.

A Matter of Expediency

"The director is on three," your secretary said efficiently.

Quickly pressing line three, you answer, "Superintendent Brown speaking."

"Jack, you been reading the papers?"

"Yes, sir. Mainly to make sure that my name is not in them."

"That's what I'm calling about. See that it stays that way. These reporters are really on our backs about overcrowding, mistreatment, recidivist rates, or any damn thing they can find. I don't have to remind you that this is an election year. The governor called me himself, and I'm calling all of the superintendents. I don't want any bad publicity. In fact, I don't want *any* publicity. And if anything unusual happens, I want to know it first. Okay?"

"You can depend on it."

That conversation took place two days ago, before the most recent incident that threatened to erupt into a very messy situation. Your mind wandered back, reviewing the events.

Nearly a hundred and fifty restless inmates had been at the Diagnostic Center for almost two weeks with nothing to do. Their days had been spent mostly standing around discussing old scores, playing basketball, lifting weights, or sleeping. One hot summer afternoon they were lined up to receive shots at the medical section. Some of the men, from the most vicious to the most agreeable, were desperately afraid of shots. Others, not so fearful, enjoyed the diversion and the discomfort of the others.

"Hey, man. I don't need no shot!"

"Go on! Stick your damn arm out. You're holding up the line," came a loud voice from the rear.

"Mind your own business. I said I don't want no shot."

One of the guards, a six-feet-four, two-hundred-seventy-five pounder, known behind his back as Hogjaw, moved over to the shot table for the third time this morning. The inmate sullenly stuck out a tattooed arm.

One old con who was getting close to the front was pale and underweight from his last trip to the outside. Booze and petty thievery had gotten him eight prison terms in three different states and an almost uncountable number of jail stints. He became more visibly frightened as each man in front of him moved on and left him waiting without hope of reprieve, one step closer to the head of the line.

In the meantime, two inmates had to be physically restrained in order for them to receive their shots, and two others had to be removed for fighting. The medical technician had taken a lot of verbal abuse, and both inmates and staff were losing patience. Eventually the old con, shaking now, reached what was to him no less formidable than a scaffold.

"What kind of shots are those?" he asked.

"Tetanus. Stick out your arm."

"I'm allergic to tetanus," he said stubbornly.

Irritated, the medical technician responded, "I've had about all of this bullshit I can take from you guys. Every damn one of you has some excuse. Stick out your arm. Now!"

"I'm allergic to tetanus."

"Officer Sistrunk."

The old con received his shot, turned around and walked three steps, and collapsed. The intern thought he had fainted, but he wasn't breathing. Frantically, they rushed him inside, out of the sight of the other inmates, and began resuscitation, but it was too late. The doctor arrived, checked the inmate's file, and found on the top of the medical jacket the hand-printed words, "allergic—tetanus." The prison doctor grabbed both the file and the medical technician and went straight to the superintendent's office.

You exploded! "This is just what I need. I can see the headlines now: 'Prisoner Dies Because Medical Technician Fails to Check Records.' Have you gotten him over to the hospital?"

"He's dead, sir."

You reached for the phone. "Miss Jenkins, get me the director."

As you outlined the situation the director interrupted, "How old is the guy?"

"Fifty-four."

"All right. I've got it. The man had a heart attack. Plain and simple, he had a heart attack."

"But it happened in front of over a hundred men."

"I don't care if it happened in front of ten thousand men. How would they know if it was a heart attack or not? He died of a heart attack!"

"The file lists the man as allergic to tetanus."

"Jack, I'm trying to keep my composure. Let me explain it for you just once: (1) destroy the record of the allergy; (2) get the man to the hospital; (3) have him declared dead of a heart attack; (4) get him buried; and (5) notify any kin that we did all that was possible—that's important. And if you can't quash this whole thing, I'll see to it that you're supervising hog feeding at the prison farm. Okay?"

"I'll take care of it," you answered uncertainly.

After hanging up, you carefully consider your options. This incident could be construed as a coverup of negligent manslaughter. However, it is very remote that such a charge would arise. In any event, who is going to worry about an eight-time loser? You have done a good job here and do not need any exaggerated criticism about one unavoidable accident. Yet you still feel uneasy about carrying out the director's instructions. Negligence has just killed a man. Mitigated, perhaps, but negligence nevertheless. The Director says heart attack. You know better. Your career could be on the line. What do you do?

INSTRUCTIONS:

Decide on a course of action.

A. Carefully define the problem.

B. List all the options or choices you can think of.

C. Rank these options in order of priority.

D. Select the option that you think is best and briefly discuss the probable consequences.

Five Practical Research Suggestions for Correctional Administrators

Daniel Glaser

My chief impression from a quarter-century of moving back and forth between correctional administration and criminological research is that these two worlds are deplorably out of touch with each other and poorly attuned to the general public. This article suggests ways in which the administrator may use research to improve both correctional services and his communication with those segments of the general public and those legislative and executive agencies of government most significant to him. Enumerating five suggestions as the topic of this article is arbitrary; these could have been subdivided and others added.

PROCURING POSTRELEASE INFORMATION

The first suggestion is simply: *Procure the most complete postrelease information obtainable on offenders in your custody or under your supervision, and work to make this information more complete.* When legislators or journalists ask for proof that specific correctional measures prevent crime, the correctional administrator is typically at a loss, having been reluctant to gather postrelease statistics because of the imperfections of any he could get. While bewailing the lack of information on recidivism, he overlooks the potential value of his own agency's records as a minimum data source.

Even a minimal tabulation from these records can begin to show whether there is a difference in postrelease crime rates for prisoners of a given type who are in different programs. Merely as a first step, it can show the number of persons released in past years who were recommitted to his correctional system. While such

Reprinted, with permission of the National Council on Crime and Delinquency, from Daniel Glaser, "Five Practical Research Suggestions for Correctional Administrators," *Crime and Delinquency,* January 1971, pp. 32-40.

information certainly does not reveal all recidivism, it imparts far more knowledge than do subjective impressions for estimating trends in recidivism rates or comparing these rates for different types of offenders or for similar offenders subjected to different types of treatment (e.g., work release, intensive vocational training, or programmed education). This is useful for any correctional administration—county, state, or national—and records can be designed to simplify such compilation.

That all criminal record information will be incomplete is inevitable, since one can know only about the offenses for which a man is caught. In all statistical comparisons, one assumes that the degree of incompleteness is approximately evenly distributed over all categories of offenders being compared. One can then examine relative postrelease criminality rates to see which categories have high rates and which lower. For example, if one can show that, among offenders of a given type, those granted work release had less criminality recorded locally two years later than those released without it, he will have a strong foothold on evaluative knowledge. Even without absolutely complete postrelease crime figures, such comparisons provide a factual basis for policy guidance. Gradually this knowledge can be improved by information covering longer follow-up periods, larger numbers of cases, more specific categories of offenders or treatments, and, ideally, a larger range of jurisdictions.

FOCUS ON COST-EFFECTIVENESS

This brings us to the second suggestion: *Focus presentation of postrelease data on the responsibilities the correctional agency must meet, especially on cost-effectiveness.* Converting a felon into a saint is a great achievement, but correctional agencies fulfill their primary responsibility if they merely reduce the probability of his committing further felonies. Even a change from felonious behavior to occasional misdemeanors represents partial success. One of the major sources of obfuscation in parole and probation outcome statistics is the counting of all types of postrelease offenses or infractions under a single label, such as parole or probation "violation." Although even nonfelonious violations disappoint those who grant parole or probation to an offender, major felonies are a much more serious disappointment to the general public.

Postrelease statistical differences between groups of offenders given special assistance and comparison groups without such aid are often much greater if expressed in terms of the amount of time which passes before violations are committed or in terms of the seriousness or persistence of violations, instead of in terms of the percentages committing violations of any kind. The variety of possible crimes and rule infractions and the diversity of their consequences for the offender are so great, however, that it is difficult to generalize about the effectiveness of correctional programs by separately enumerating every type of posttreatment maladjustment. Nevertheless, a single index which reflects both time before violation and seriousness is the percentage of time spent reconfined in a given postrelease period. Therefore, an administrator may most effectively contrast a special treatment group with a control or comparison group not by their gross violation rates but by their average total months of reconfinement in a given number of years after release.

A major advantage of this index is that it can easily be expressed in terms of *cost* of reconfinement per postrelease year, decade, or other period. This has been shown most effectively by Stuart Adams in his report on the PICO Project, and in his subsequent research. Since prison treatment in most systems costs approximately ten times as much as supervision in the community, an administrator can present strong economic justification for any extra expenditures which reduce the time of reconfinement for a given group of offenders in a postrelease period. If one thousand dollars of reconfinement costs are saved by five hundred dollars for added community services that reduce reincarceration, there is a one hundred percent return on investment. This is not to imply that economy is the major moral argument for a correctional program, but reconfinement time during a postrelease period is about as satisfactory a statistical index as one can obtain to indicate a society's total moral outrage with a group of released offenders. Furthermore, in these days of government financial stress, cutting costs is a crucial and persuasive consideration, particularly in the many states with antiquated and regressive taxation systems.

ECONOMIC PROBLEMS OF RELEASEES

This point is also relevant to my third suggestion: *The economic problems of releasees can be remedied if they are known.* It is relatively meaningless to argue that the economic reasons for recidivism are more important than the psychological or that either are more important than social or cultural reasons. Certainly all are intertwined, and a good criminological theory would generalize on the nature of their interrelationship. Suffice it to note here (1) that we can demonstrate statistically a close relationship between economic hardship and crime in the careers of most felons and (2) that unemployment is closely related to crime, especially among adult offenders. One should also note that over 90 percent of felonies reported to the police involve the taking of someone's money or property. Furthermore, unlike more abstractly conceived psychological problems, the economic dilemmas of ordinary people can be understood, without special training, by almost everyone.

It is surprising that correctional literature almost completely ignores the economic difficulties of men released from confinement. What evidence we have suggests that this problem limits correctional effectiveness much more than does the size of caseloads or the shortage of psychiatrists. Though acute economic need does not characterize all releasees, the massive statistical dimensions of the economic problem must be a vital consideration in any overall effort to make correctional investments more fruitful.

Studies indicate that about a third of federal parolees and mandatory releasees find no work in their first month out of prison, and a sixth find none for three months after release. Furthermore, since whatever work they may get at first is often temporary and followed by unemployment, a quarter were without jobs when contacted during their third month after release. Almost half the federal releasees earned less than fifty dollars during their first month out of prison. Fortunately, the majority of releasees receive some assistance with room and board from their families, but this is not a satisfactory solution for long. Considering the clothing and other possessions that most newly released prisoners lack, their financial needs in many ways exceed those of men never confined. Considering also the combination of low income, limited resources, accumulated needs, pent-up desires, and prior criminality, it is remarkable that at least nine out of ten adult offenders spend at least their first month out of prison trying to solve their problems by legitimate means; in most jurisdictions for which data are available, a majority seem to persist indefinitely.

Data from research on the postrelease economic problems of federal parole and mandatory release violators have helped promote several postprison assistance measures, such as increased funds for release gratuities and an added number of employment placement officers, prison employees whose sole function is to seek jobs for releasees. But by far the most significant development for economic and other aid was the creation of the Federal Community Correction Centers in New York, Chicago, Detroit, Los Angeles, and a half-dozen other cities, to which federal offenders are transferred about three months before they start parole.

Prisoners residing in these centers go out to seek jobs, start to work at those they procure, and visit their future homes before moving out to begin parole. A full-time employment counselor aids the twenty to thirty residents of each center. These programs create a dramatic increase in employment rates for youthful recidivist parolees, and the follow-up studies thus far show an especially great drop in this group's postrelease felonies. Counseling a youth about job-getting on the very day he is to seek employment, or on job-holding when he is concerned about this, is much more effective than counseling him about hypothetical postrelease situations while he is still in prison. Gradual departure from prison thus permits prisoners of all ages to organize their postrelease life much more adequately than when they must move abruptly from being completely cared for in a prison to being entirely on their own, with limited resources, in the city.

Perhaps the major contribution of community correction centers, work release, or work furlough is one least often cited—their diagnostic value. Traditionally, the duration of confinement is determined by the judge's interpretation of presentence information and later by the parole board's assessment of this information plus additional reports from prison personnel. Such decisions are tested, however, by the released offender's noncriminality in the community. The economic, personality, and social problems of those endeavoring to support themselves legitimately and the criminal inclinations of others are much more quickly evident to staff in these graduated release programs than in either the artificial environment of the prison or the formal and infrequent contacts of regular probation or parole supervision. Graduated release programs protect the public not just by aiding rehabilitation but also by providing more immediate and relevant surveillance than is possible in other correctional programs. That is why federal judges are relying increasingly on community centers as places for thirty to ninety days of presentence study in cases where they are uncertain whether to impose probation or imprisonment.

ADDRESSING THE OFFENDER'S TOTAL CIRCUMSTANCES AND PERSPECTIVES

Despite the statistically frequent importance of economic conditions, tracing thoroughly the chain of events culminating in any individual's return to crime usually provides support for my fourth suggestion: *Both correctional administration and research should try to comprehend the total circumstances of an offender's current situation and his view of these circumstances.* For example, some releasees are successfully placed in jobs but are too lonely and restless when not at work to resist the ease and welcome they can find in drug use, heavy drinking, or professional criminal social circles. More familiar and accepting companions are especially attractive to them in any period of discomfort, humiliation, conflict, or other stress or when they are required to deal with bureaucratic, more educated, or ethnically different persons at work, in probation or parole offices, and elsewhere. Solutions to economic problems may be necessary for most offenders, but they are not sufficient to prevent recidivism in all.

While research indicates that the majority of ex-prisoners who return to felonies do so only after some effort to "make it on the legit," there is also a significant minority whose perceptions of their competence and prospects in criminal activity are so great that they disdain from the start, or soon thereafter, what they view as their legitimate alternatives to crime. For them a drastic change of experience at legitimate pursuits—in learning and using a skilled trade, for example—may be possible only with long confinement in an optimum program and extensively graduated release. Contrastingly, another noteworthy minority have so predominantly identified themselves with anticriminal persons before their arrest, are so deterred from crime by their arrest and penalty, and have so little prospect of further ties with criminals if released abruptly that most correctional measures—including graduated release—are either irrelevant or somewhat deleterious to their high prospects of nonrecidivism.

What is suggested here is a prescriptive penology which varies both assistance and control with the offender. But this implies learning and taking into account the offender's view of his world at the times that are critical to him. To do so requires changing the qualifications and functions of correctional personnel in both institutions and community-based services. A sound prescription requires that the view of the client be based less exclusively on office interviews or formal test scores and more on familiarity with his daily social circumstances, reactions, and expectations, around the clock, in *his* usual situations.

In federal prison research we asked inmates to think of the prison employee whom they liked best and to bear him in mind while we asked questions about him, but not to reveal his name. We then asked several questions about this person, including the type of position he held. We repeated this inquiry regarding the prison employee the inmate disliked the most. One of our findings was the great predominance of work supervisors among prison employees most liked. Although another finding indicated that prison caseworkers were the most disliked more often than the most liked, they did not compose a high percentage of either designation. The data suggest that work supervisors and line custodial officers have much more impact on inmates than do caseworkers, and I infer that this is because their relationships with inmates are more continuous, cooperative, and personal than those of caseworkers. This was dramatically indicated by studies of successful releasees from prison who were asked to trace their change from criminal to noncriminal concerns. About half said that they changed during imprisonment, about half of these credited a staff member as the most influential person in this change, and in over half of these cases the staff member so credited was a work supervisor.

On the basis of this interpretation it was suggested that caseworkers (1) cease segregating their offices within a single part of the prison and, instead, scatter them, each in a separate work or residence unit of the prison, to make them more accessible to inmates and better located for observation of prison life; (2) cease to have inmates assigned to them randomly from all over the institution and, instead, have caseloads comprised of all inmates assigned to the units where their office is located so that they may more readily know all parties in the social relationships of their clients; (3) each serve as part of a classification team consisting primarily of line officers from these units, but with some representation from prison school, industry, and management, to replace the traditional single institution classification committee of top prison officials, who necessarily must meet hastily and infrequently on most inmates.

The measures described above have now been adopted, with variations, in many federal and state correctional institutions. They bring much more spontaneity, frankness, and even affection to many inmate-caseworker relationships. Classification teams not only meet several times as often on the average inmate as do institution classification committees and operate with more thorough knowledge of the inmates but also greatly enhance communication among the various components of the prison staff. While it would be naive to assume that these measures permit staff to address the *total* prison circumstances of each inmate, they certainly increase the proportion of these circumstances that staff are likely to take into account.

As already indicated, graduated release programs give correctional staff a fuller and more immediate knowledge of the offender's community situation than is usually possible wth abrupt release to parole or probation. In the latter, the officer's opportunity to know his caseload more thoroughly might conceivably be enhanced by reduced caseloads, but time studies and controlled experiments suggest that reduced caseloads tend to increase time in paperwork more than in fieldwork, and in presentence more than in postsentence activity. A partial remedy, pioneered in Chicago, is decentralization of parole and probation offices from a single downtown center to scattered neighborhood units, each housing a variety of municipal, county, state, and private correctional, law enforcement, and social service agencies. This facilitates their collaboration, and also permits, through some sharing of staff and files, provision of some personnel for night and weekly duty.

The most adequate solutions to the problem of addressing the total circumstances of offenders stress three specific goals: (1) *supplementing professional casework staff with paraprofessionals of the same sociocultural and neighborhood background as the clients;* (2) *directing assistance at the entire family of the offender;* (3) *being available for crisis alleviation twenty-four hours a day, seven days a week.*

One way of approaching these goals is exemplified by the Probation Officer-

Case Aide Project of the U.S. Probation Office in Chicago. The probation officers in this project have part-time aides who are available in the clients' own neighborhoods during evenings and weekends. Frequently ex-offenders themselves, the aides are of the same background as their clients and, in the one to three cases to which they are assigned, can readily become familiar with the clients' total life styles and reputations and offer immediate assistance. In emergencies they can telephone the probation officer at the latter's home, but they routinely make automatically tape-recorded phone calls to the probation office to report their observations and activities on each case.

A more thorough approach to these three goals is represented by the "RO-DEO" project, an acronym for Reduction of Delinquency through Expansion of Opportunity, of the Los Angeles County Probation Department. Here each probation officer has two full-time paraprofessional aides from the neighborhood. Each three-man team serves no more than thirty juvenile offenders who would traditionally have been institutionalized. Offices for these teams are in the clients' neighborhood and include space for community meetings. The teams treat the entire family of each client. They may help the parents get employment, welfare service, or medical assistance and often also transport them to the offices involved. They may provide emergency baby-sitting or pitch in to help a mother clean up her apartment as a first step in teaching her how to handle her household problems. The emphasis is on helping all family members learn to cope more successfully with a difficult environment, as well as with medical, educational, or other handicaps.

Appropriately titled "Community Workers," the RODEO project's aides to probation officers now have civil service status. They are given considerable responsibility and autonomy as they demonstrate their capacity for it. When the program began, early in 1967, it was centered in a predominantly black area encompassing Watts, but after it demonstrated marked success in reducing confinement costs, it was expanded to include an office in predominantly Mexican-American East Los Angeles and is currently being further augmented by two new offices in integrated areas. Its original supervisor, Mrs. Ruth L. Rushen, is now applying its principles to the still larger area of the Model Neighborhood Program and to probationers of all ages. This new program is called "Harambee," Swahili for "Let us all work together."

PROPOSE CHANGES AS PIECEMEAL EXPERIMENTS

This brings us to my fifth suggestion: *Correctional improvement proposals will be most readily supported if they are introduced piecemeal and include procedures for measuring effectiveness.*

The major source of knowledge in medicine, the most rigorously scientific of treatment sciences, is the controlled experiment. Where randomly selected experimental and control groups with double-blind procedures have not been feasible, medicine has relied on quasi-experimental comparisons of similar people receiving different treatment due to different circumstances in former periods or other areas. Rigorously controlled experiments are possible in correction more often than is usually assumed, but where they are not feasible, the quasi-experimental use of comparison groups can improve knowledge greatly if a minimum of appropriately standardized and concise records is maintained. The records most valuable for evaluating a program can also be the most efficient and useful for correctional operations. Planning and pretesting of standardized, efficient, and relevant records should be part of the first stage in any new correctional program, rather than an afterthought, just as a bookkeeping system should be established when a business begins, rather than later when one wonders where the money went.

Without appropriate records and their analysis by an approximation of the experimental method, any argument on the effectiveness of a correctional program is no more conclusive than a statement of one man's impressions against another's. Legislators and executives in control of government expenditures for coping with crime obviously are not convinced that any group of experts has a guaranteed solution for these problems. In recent years federal and state agencies have granted money for innovations only when the measures were proposed as small-scale experiments with planned evaluation. Research is prominent today in all fields, and legislators can be readily persuaded of the value of correctional research if its prospects for expanding knowledge on crime control are made reasonably clear.

For those correctional administrators who think they know what they need to make their services more effective, a government which vetoes proposals for new programs can be frustrating. But administrators who follow the five suggestions set forth here will, I believe, by justifying their financial requests more adequately, become better able to procure necessary funds.

Selected Bibliography

AMOS, WILLIAM E. "The Philosophy of Corrections: Revisited." *Federal Probation,* 38(1974):43–46.

BURNS, HENRY JR. *Corrections Organization and Administration.* St. Paul, Minn.: West Publishing Co., 1975.

CARTER, ROBERT; GLASER, DANIEL; and WILKINS, LESLIE T. *Correctional Institutions.* 2d ed., Philadelphia: J.B. Lippincott Co., 1977.

CARTWRIGHT, DESMOND S.; HUNTER, ROBERT M.; HOWARD, KATHERINE; and HUIZINGA, DAVID. "Hierarchical Management Monitoring." *Criminology,* 12(1974):25–51.

COHEN, YONA. "Staff Supervision in Probation." *Federal Probation,* 40(1976):17–23.

COUGHLIN, JOSEPH S.; GRUENDEL, GEORGE F., and SHAY, DONALD E. "The Zero-Base Budget As a Management Tool." *Federal Probation,* 41(1977):39–42.

DAUBER, EDWARD, and SCHICHOR, DAVID. "A Comparative Exploration of Prison Discipline." *Journal of Criminal Justice,* 7(1979):21–37.

FOGEL, DAVID. *We Are The Living Proof. . . ,* Cincinnati: Anderson Publishing Co., 1975.

FOGEL, DAVID. "The Politics of Corrections." *Federal Probation,* 41(1977):27–31.

GIBBONS, DON D.; and BLAKE, GERALD F. "Program Evaluation In Correction." *Crime and Delinquency,* 22(1976):309–321.

GLASER, DANIEL. "Five Practical Research Suggestions for Correctional Administrators." *Crime and Delinquency,* 17(1971):32–40.

HOGAN, CORNELIUS D., and STEINHURST, WILLIAM R. "Managing Change in Corrections." *Federal Probation,* 40(1976):55–59.

JOHNSON, ELMER H. "A Basic Error: Dealing with Inmates As Though They Were Abnormal." *Federal Probation,* 19(1971):39–44.

JOHNSTON, NORMAN. *The Human Cage: A Brief History of Prison Architecture.* New York: Walter and Company, 1973.

KILLINGER, GEORGE C., and CROMWELL, PAUL F. *Penology*. St. Paul, Minn.: West Publishing Co., 1973.

LANSING, DOUGLAS; BOGAN, JOSEPH; and KARACKI, LOVEN. "Unit Management: Implementing a Different Correctional Approach." *Federal Probation*, 41(1977):43–49.

LEAVITT, ALAN. "The High Art of Staff Leadership." *Federal Probation*, 38(1974):30–33.

MENNINGER, KARL. *The Crime of Punishment*. New York: Viking, 1968.

MURPHY, PATRICK J. "The Team Concept." *Federal Probation*, 39(1975):30–34.

NAGEL, WILLIAM G. *The New Red Barn: A Critical Look at the Modern American Prison*. New York: Walker and Company, 1973.

NELSON, CARL W. "Cost-Benefit Analysis and Alternatives to Incarceration." *Federal Probation*, 39(1973):45–50.

ROTHMAN, DAVID J. *The Discovery of the Asylum*. Boston: Little, Brown, 1971.

RUBIN, SOL. *Rubin's Law of Criminal Correction*. 2d ed., St. Paul, Minn.: West Publishing Co., 1973.

SINGER, NEIL M. "Economic Implications of Standards for Correctional Institutions." *Crime and Delinquency*, 23(1977):14–31.

SCHRINK, JEFF. "Strategy for Preparing Correctional Reports." *Federal Probation*, 40(1976):33–40.

WALDO, GORDON P. "Myths, Misconceptions and the Misuse of Statistics in Correctional Research." *Crime and Delinquency*, 17(1971):57–66.

WALDRON, RONALD J. "Correctional Administration: Employee Promotions." *Federal Probation*, 41(1977):49–54.

WATERS, J. EUGENE. "Perceived Environments: A Sociological Description of the Correctional Setting." *Southern Journal of Criminal Justice*, 3(1978):17–25.

VANAGUNAS, STANLEY. "National Standards and Goals on Corrections: Some Issues of Implementation." *Criminology*, 14(1976):233–240.